Y0-DUM-181

# ELEMENTS OF MODERN MANAGEMENT

# ELEMENTS OF MODERN MANAGEMENT

**EUGENE J. BENGE**

and the editors of
Alexander Hamilton Institute

amacom
A DIVISION OF AMERICAN MANAGEMENT ASSOCIATIONS

**Library of Congress Cataloging in Publication Data**

Benge, Eugene J
Elements of modern management.

Includes index.
1. Industrial management. I. Alexander Hamilton Institute, New York. II. Title.
HD31.B388 658.4 76-25179
ISBN 0-8144-5428-3



Third printing

# PREFACE

Since the middle sixties, many influences have catalyzed important advances in management practices.

Probably the strongest influence has been the changing attitudes toward work of the younger people in the work force. Increasingly, managers have had to cope with labor shortages for low status jobs, turnover, absenteeism, and disregard for quality. But are the younger workers alone the cause of these problems? Or have management practices created attitudes that contributed to the problems?

Some sociologists assert that extreme subdivision of work, which results in monotonous, uninteresting jobs, is largely responsible for the present situation.

Inflation has been another potent force, sharply raising the costs of raw materials and equipment. Employees and unions have demanded higher wages to meet a rising cost of living, so contributing to "cost-push" inflation. Worldwide shortages of many basic materials have added "demand-pull" inflation.

Government has tried wage and price controls with little success. Legislators have passed restrictive laws on employee-employer relations, working conditions, safety, pensions, ecology, mergers, and other management actions.

Old management attitudes and practices are no longer adequate for a socio-politico-industrial economy. This book endeavors to point out the practices which modern managers are developing to meet the new conditions. It even attempts to give an occasional peek through the keyhole of the present into the great murky void which we call the future.

A special contribution to the preparation of this book has been made by the editors of the Alexander Hamilton Institute of New York. For more than 65 years the Institute has gathered and disseminated vast amounts of management information. I am particularly impressed with its efforts in recent years to provide important information about U.S. business practices to internationally minded executives throughout the world.

Inevitably, my association with members of the Institute's staff has been reflected in the writing of this book. In addition, its editors have made specific suggestions that I have incorporated. I am grateful to them for their collaboration and guidance.

*Eugene J. Benge*

# CONTENTS

# 1

# MANAGEMENT MOVES AHEAD

Many people think that management is a relatively new practice, something that arrived on the scene in the eighteenth or nineteenth century. Actually the practice of management dates back to the time when people first banded together. There is much physical evidence of the results produced by managers at work, evidence that extends back tens of thousands of years.

All outstanding projects have required planning and direction, regardless of when they were carried out. King Solomon built his great Temple in the tenth century B.C. Centuries earlier, in Egypt, various forward-looking pharaohs constructed pyramids as their personal tombs. The Greeks built the Parthenon 2,500 years ago. The Romans erected Hadrian's wall in northern England around 120 A.D. The Notre Dame Cathedral was completed about 1208 and the Panama Canal in 1914. The United States put a man on the moon in 1969. All these projects needed managers and management.

However, while management has been practiced since the earliest groupings of man, what is new is the *way* it is practiced. Obviously, the kind of management needed for erecting Solomon's Temple was vastly different from that which helped to rocket men to the moon. Yet both projects had certain elements in common:

A major objective and subobjectives were set.

Procedures for accomplishing them were established.

The necessary human and material resources were organized.

Directions to workers of all levels were issued throughout the activity.

Efforts were coordinated as to time and place.

Control was exercised to insure that all elements were completed at the times and places planned.

Over many centuries one man at the top made all important decisions. His word was law, and woe to him who did not perform. The lowest workers were slaves or serfs. Middle managers ranged from slave drivers to confidants of the autocratic ruler.

This authoritarian kind of management lasted into the nineteenth century, even after feudalism had disappeared and the industrial revolution had arrived. Cracking the whip was thought to be the only way to get important projects done. For example, in 1840 a plantation owner opened up a cotton mill in South Carolina. Twenty-five years later his son, and 50 years later his grandson, carried on the business in much the same autocratic fashion as the founder. This was family management, a quite usual form of authoritarian management.

## The Industrial Revolution

In the middle of the eighteenth century, mechanization of industrial production took hold—first in England, later in other countries—and wiped out the few remnants of feudalism and "cottage production." Spinning thread and weaving cloth, once done in the home, were gradually transferred to the factory, where machines produced more cloth than a handicraft system could. Workers, fearful of the new order, at first rioted and destroyed the looms, but gradually accepted the factory system of production.

Other inventions hastened the Industrial Revolution—the cotton gin, the steam engine, the reaper, the telegraph, improvements in the printing press. Necessarily, these innovations wrought great social change.

Managers readily adopted the factory system but continued the same authoritarian kind of direction that had characterized leadership for many centuries. Child labor was accepted. Adult workers receiving low wages eked out an existence. Working conditions were bad. With increasing mechanization, industrial accidents rose.

In the last decades of the nineteenth century a new form of ownership came into use: the corporation. It differed from individual ownership and partnership in several respects:

- It was a legal entity, which could be sued or otherwise held accountable for its actions.
- Officers (and to a limited but increasing extent elected directors) bore legal responsibility for corporate actions.
- Professional management came into being, theoretically responsible to stockholders but sometimes self-serving and self-perpetuating.
- The corporation amassed capital for production and marketing in amounts generally not possible for individual owners.

Although early corporations often exploited people and resources, they also undoubtedly made possible an increasing standard of living, which in turn ultimately permitted the development of mass production for mass markets. Even Karl Marx, father of communism, grudgingly wrote of capitalism, "During its rule of scarce one hundred years, it has created . . . more colossal productive forces than have all preceding generations together." Since the late nineteenth century, the capitalist system has grown at an accelerating rate. The wise investment of capital by competent management has been largely responsible for this growth.

## Five Phases of Management Evolution

An overview suggests that management has evolved through five stages: authoritarian management, scientific management, human relations management, results oriented management, and social responsibility management. Although the transitions have been so gradual that each stage merges into the next almost imperceptibly, the approximate dates of transition can be identified. New trends in management are added to the past. They may alter the previous approaches but do not necessarily discard them. Figure 1 illustrates the evolution of management and shows the great changes which have come about in this century. The dates selected are approximate

*Figure 1. Kinds of management since the beginning of mankind.*

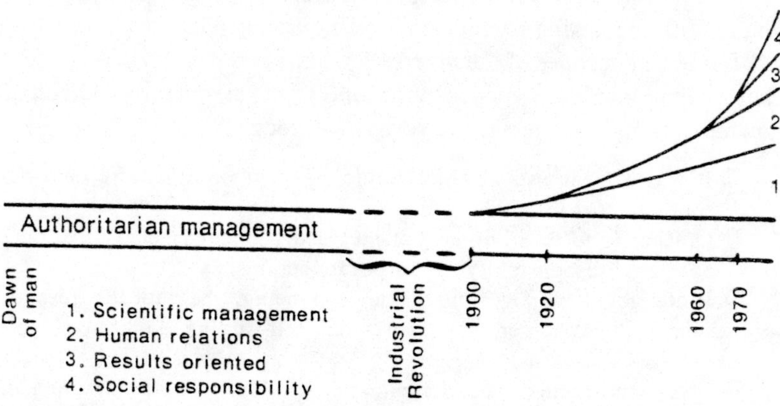


and indicate when each concept began to achieve wide acceptance.

Some characteristics of the earliest stage, authoritarian management, have already been discussed. As long as the judgment of the top man was sound and employees accepted his leadership without question, that system produced excellent results. Since power corrupts, the system also produced some robber barons of industry—ruthless men who exploited others to make themselves fabulously rich. Moreover, authoritarian management was frequently trial-and-error management. Subordinates struggled to find some way—any way—to carry out the demands of the Big Boss. The solutions this system produced were not necessarily the best possible as scientific management later demonstrated.

## Scientific Management

Around the turn of the century, a few engineers in the United States and Europe began to seek new ways of performing work or managing an enterprise. The movement came to be known as "scientific management."

Early hints of scientific management are found in the work of three British industrialists: James Watt, Jr. (1769-1848), son of one of the developers of the steam engine; Robert Owen (1771-1858), a social reformer and philanthropist; and Charles Babbage (1792-1871), a scientist and mathematician.

Pioneer American and foreign contributors to the movement included, among others:

Ernest Solvay (1838-1922) of Belgium
Henri Fayol (1841-1925) of France
Henry R. Towne (1844-1924) of the United States
James Rowan (1851-1906) of Great Britain
Harrington Emerson (1853-1931) of the United States
Carl G. L. Barth (1860-1939) of the United States
Henry L. Gantt (1861-1919) of the United States
Karol Adamiecki (1866-1933) of Poland
Walter Rathenau (1867-1922) of Germany
Mary P. Follett (1868-1933) of the United States
Frank B. Gilbreth (1868-1924) of the United States
Wallace Clark (1880-1948) of the United States
G. Elton Mayo (1880-1949) of Australia

But an American, Frederick Winslow Taylor (1856-1915), is generally regarded as the father of scientific management. The new approach which he developed profoundly affected the practice of management. Radical in its day, it is now considered orthodox and authoritarian. Many of its devices have been superseded by newer methods, but most of its basic principles still hold.

Taylor believed two attitudes to be the essence of scientific management:

1. Both management and workers needed to take their eyes off the division of the surplus and to turn their attention toward increasing its size.

2. Both needed to substitute exact scientific investigation and knowledge for individual judgment or opinion on workers' tasks.

The principal devices developed by scientific management have been:

Time and motion study, resulting in work standards.
Incentive pay for achieving tasks set.
Functional foremanship (specialists).
Planning and scheduling, instruction cards, slide rules, tables.
Standardization of methods, tools, and parts.
Production costing.
Purchasing by specifications and bids.
Production control systems, including graphic methods.

Practitioners of scientific management ultimately added numerous refinements and techniques to these basics. Consider briefly the different contributions of Henri Fayol and the Gilbreths.

Henri Fayol, a French contemporary of Taylor, made some profound contributions to management thinking. Unfortunately his writings were not translated into English until 1929.

Fayol pointed out that the job of manager at successively higher levels becomes less technical and more managerial. He developed the concept which is now called administration: the managerial functions of planning, organizing, command (direction), and coordination and control. He believed that the whole process of management could be taught in universities and within companies, in much the same way as technical information. Thus, he antedated the executive development movement by a half-century.

Frank Gilbreth and his wife, Lillian (1878-1972), made great additions to scientific management through their studies of worker motions. Frank reduced the motions of a bricklayer from 18 to 5 and almost trebled the number of bricks laid per day. After his death in 1924, Lillian carried on his work for several decades.

In the early days of motion study, lights were placed on a worker's hand, elbow, or head, and a photograph was taken which revealed the motions as streaks of light. This type of photograph was termed a "cyclograph." From this simple beginning there evolved other useful devices for recording motions and times: the microchronometer, a stereoscopic motion picture camera, a cross-sectional background for measuring distances traveled, 17 elementary motions called "therbligs," and "simultaneous motion cycle" charts. Disciples of Gilbreth have added other refinements to time and motion economy methods.

### Scientific Management from 1910 to 1960

Between 1910 and 1960 scientific management bore fruit. Its influence in the United States is reflected to some extent in the following figures, which represent its standing in percent of world totals:

| U.S. Percent of World: | 1910 | 1960 |
|---|---|---|
| Population | 5% | 6% |
| Wealth | 15% | 50% |
| Income | 15% (est.) | 35% |

Of course, these increases in the period 1910–1960 resulted from a number of favorable factors, but scientific management must be considered among the most important of them.

Other nations are currently outgrowing rigid scientific management and adopting more advanced techniques, technology, and management practices. So it is not likely that the years 1960 to 2010 will continue the trends at the same high levels.

Over the 1910–1960 period, money was the main work incentive. Piece rates and various task and bonus plans were developed but soon caused discontent because of resulting pay inequities. For hourly-wage and salaried occupations, two systems of job evaluation gained wide acceptance—point systems and the factor comparison method. Merit rating evolved into performance appraisal, used principally with salaried employees. Both job evaluation and performance appraisal were applied upward to supervisory, technical, and even managerial personnel, usually with good results.

Over this half-century, military science was developing rapidly. It included studies of organization and organization relationships.

**Military Influence on Scientific Management**

World War I exercised considerable influence on scientific management along three distinct lines:

1. Speedup of production and development of production technology.
2. Adoption by industrial managers of some concepts of military science.
3. New concepts in personnel selection, training, and supervision.

It was a period of world upheavål. In the United States, shipyards and munitions plants recruited labor from farms, offices, and stores and from other plants. Housewives became lathe hands and welders. Labor rates escalated. Raw materials and housing were scarce. War orders went to companies poorly equipped to handle them. And, as always in wartime, inflation reared its ugly head.

In such a setting, changes in the practice of management, including the three major effects listed above, were inevitable. Later chapters will show how such changes were superimposed on scientific management during and since World War I.

## Establishment of Management Societies

By the onset of World War I, managers had become class conscious, and the term "management profession" began to be used. In 1911 the Society to Promote the Science of Management was organized. Following Frederick Winslow Taylor's death, in 1915, it was renamed the Taylor Society. In 1936 it merged with the Society of Industrial Engineers, founded in 1917, to form the Society for Advancement of Management (SAM).

The American Management Associations (AMA) was founded in 1923, an outgrowth of several organizations. After a struggle for survival during the Great Depression of the thirties, it became a large, financially successful organization for training in varied aspects of management. Ultimately, it took SAM under its wing.

Recent decades have seen a proliferation of societies dedicated to specialized aspects of management: quality control, industrial engineering, plant maintenance, marketing, advertising, packaging, office work, computerization, cybernetics, industrial relations, and scores of others. All these organizations add to the growing body of knowledge available to managers.

## Human Relations in Management

By the beginning of World War I, "Taylorism" had attracted many devotees, some of whom were more interested in making a fast buck than in genuine applications of scientific management. Some managers used time study and other devices to exploit workers. Before many years the new "efficiency work" fell into disrepute. Organized labor was one of its strongest opponents.

The American Federation of Labor (AFL) had been organized in 1886 by Samuel Gompers. It consisted largely of skilled craftsmen. By the turn of the century its voice was being heard on wages, hours, and working conditions for its members.

In the early 1900s Hugo Munsterberg, a German-born Harvard psychologist, was pointing out applications of psychology to everyday living. Others were experimenting with psychological tests for career guidance, a field which received great emphasis during World War I when several million inductees were given psychological tests.

In the decade before World War I, the welfare of working people began receiving greater attention, a trend that has accelerated to the present day. Society in general, and lawmakers in particular, began to believe that big business was exploiting labor and the consumer. Laws were enacted to stop child labor, to compensate workers injured in industrial accidents, to improve working conditions and to safeguard employee health.

Following World War I, management became more conscious of its human relations problems and obligations and appointed new specialists to handle them. But these specialists, known as "personnel managers," soon discovered that their effectiveness was limited; they had, in fact, little authority to stop many of the practices which were causing employee discontent.

Between 1920 and 1960, managers began to realize that labor relations was a full-scale management problem. These years included a great economic depression, World War II, and the Korean War. Both the AFL and the Congress of Industrial Organizations (CIO) grew in membership and became more militant. Laws and administrative bodies such as the National Labor Relations Board severely restricted management actions in supervising labor and in collective bargaining. Writers and academicians criticized management handling of employee relations.

Management of course was sensitive to such pressures and for the most part responded positively to them. As a result, the 1920–1960 period can be characterized as "the period of awakening management attention to human relations," attention which persists to this day.

## Results Oriented Management

The concept of results oriented management, or management by results, was developed in the 1960s, primarily in reaction to an increasingly apparent failing of scientific management. Scientific management stressed methodology: time standards, pay plans, work schedules, job descriptions, analyses of costs, and the like. The emphasis was on *activities*, both of workers and supervisors. Job titles on organization charts reflected this accent. However, activities did not always bring results, and sometimes failure merely meant more of the same type of activity. Annual reports by department managers were largely summarizations of actions.

For example, the author was once assigned to examine the work of a research and development department in a medium-size paper company. The manager was proud of his department's record: In a period of several years, three new products had been developed, and four others were expected to be completed "within a year or two." However, investigation showed clearly that only one of the seven products stood a chance of paying its research costs, let alone of becoming commercially profitable. The prevalence of such misguided emphasis on activities rather than results set the stage for the general acceptance of the concept of results oriented management. The concept will be examined in later chapters.

## Social Responsibility Management

Currently a new dimension is being added to the scope of management: social responsibility. Public opinion, employee pressures, and legislative requirements make it clear that society expects more from management than products and profits. So this trend, too, will be discussed in later chapters.

Change in our industrial system is but one part of a social revolution, the end of which is not yet in sight. All of man's great social institutions are affected: government, education, religion, capitalism, and even the most basic unit, the family.

The signs of this revolution are many: youth dissatisfaction, employee turnover, race riots, sexual freedom, the hippie movement, drugs, bizarre technology, antireligious cynicism. The international scene has witnessed the toppling of monarchies, the rising expectations of new nations, two world wars, communications via man-made satellites, space travel, the rise of ecology, and the breakdown of international monetary systems. Obviously the future cannot be a straight-line extrapolation of the past nor a reversion to any former social order.

Production is the warp on which the woof of any society's fabric is woven. Management is the force that brings together the various elements for production: raw materials, workers, equipment, know-how. Managers must play important roles in future social change.

## INNOVATIONS AFFECT MANAGEMENT

Innovation, whether social or technological, may cause as many problems as it claims to solve. Many well-intentioned governmental programs discover this harsh reality. In business some typical results of innovation may be:

- First-time problems may arise. For routine tasks, traditional bureaucratic, vertical, line management works reasonably well. For first-time problems, the challenge of rapid change or emergencies, orthodox management often reacts poorly or merely offers unreasonable resistance.
- Changes in internal organization relationships frequently occur.
- Unless wide-scope planning and stage-setting accompany innovation, confusing temporary expedients may be used in an attempt to link the past with the future.
- Employees, managers, suppliers, and customers may find difficulty adjusting to new conditions brought about by innovation.

In short, technological innovations have social side effects. Mankind introduces television, nuclear energy, birth control pills, or electronic computers with little thought to social consequences.

Managers are often guilty of the same kind of negligence. They purchase new equipment or set up new procedures without planning for the adjustments employees will have to make. Wise managers, when contemplating drastic change, involve employees and supervisors in discussions about the need for change and about possible courses of action. In this way employees are prepared for the innovation and may even be eager for its benefits.

Yesterday's manager conformed to the organization structure, lines of authority, rules, and goals assigned to him. Rewards came from the organization itself, not from his own feeling of worthiness or from influences outside the company.

The new manager thinks of himself as a professional, especially if he is technically trained. He associates himself with other professionals in his particular area of competence. He works for an employer for salary and security but voluntarily labors in the garden of his chosen field. He will change to another employer more readily than to another kind of work. So, he is mobile, and is less loyal to the employer than was the manager of the past. His rewards come from satisfying accomplishment, contributions to his field, or the respect of peers in that field. His commitment is to his chosen career. However, his break with tradition has also made him susceptible to greater stress.

Worldwide, business managers are being subjected to critical scrutiny and even attack. People and governments fear the financial and economic power which is concentrated in large industrial organizations, especially multinational companies.

In most industrialized nations, changing attitudes toward work reflect rising affluence. Nonmaterial values are becoming more important.

Managers face a triple challenge: (1) to produce more and better goods, (2) to improve the environment and other conditions of life, and (3) to adapt to great changes in the political and economic environment. To meet this challenge, managerial statesmanship is needed.

## GLOSSARY

Throughout this book a number of terms will be used to describe specific aspects of management, and it will be worthwhile to refer to definitions of such terms now, at the outset. A few of the definitions may not be clear at this point. Refer to this glossary again when these terms are used in later chapters.

**Accountability.** The obligation of a subordinate to report to his superior when exercising authority and performing assigned duties.

**Administration.** A management function which includes planning, organizing, directing, coordinating, and control of work.

**Authority.** The power to control the human, material, and financial resources needed to discharge responsibilities; and the right to make decisions pertinent to them.

**Centralization.** The retention of authority and responsibility by a manager. Compare *decentralization.*

**Chain of command.** The chain of reporting relationships which results from delegating and redelegating authority and responsibility to successively lower levels.

**Communication.** The transmission of understanding and motivation from one person to another.

**Control.** Establishment of performance standards for a plan and the evaluation of performance of those responsible for carrying it out.

**Coordination.** The integration of space, time, energy, and material elements to provide unified action in carrying out a plan.

**Decentralization.** The process of extending authority and/or responsibility to lower organization levels.

**Delegation.** The act of transferring selected responsibilities, with commensurate authority, to one or more subordinates.

**Direction.** The words or actions of a manager which designate to subordinates who is to do what, and when.

**Diversification.** The process of increasing the variety of existing products and/or services.

**Duties.** The physical, mental, and social activities required of an employee by his job.

**Fringe benefits.** Various forms of compensation to employees, other than pay.

**Function.** A division of the total management task which groups related activities; it usually is preceded by a descriptive adjective.

**Goal.** A clearly defined end, aim, objective, or target, preferably one that is measurable.

**Line employee.** One who has a nonsupervisory job in a primary function of an organization. Compare *staff employee.*

**Management.** The activities required for setting up or administering an organization.

**Management information system.** An organized procedure to supply executives with information pertinent to their assignments.

**Management science.** The application of the scientific method and mathematics to the study of management problems.

**Manager.** One who carries out management activities.

**Method.** The traditional or prescribed way to perform a given task.

**Organization.** The structure that results from subdividing work into functions and jobs, and the planned interrelationships among these parts.

**Organization chart.** A graphic device which shows job titles, names of job holders, and reporting relationships of line, staff, and supervisory employees.

**Planning.** The process of determining goals and procedures; usually this means determining what, how, when, where, and who.

**Policy.** A standing decision for a recurring problem, subject to change as conditions demand.

**Procedure.** The sequential steps for performance of a repetitive task.

**Responsibility.** The obligation to perform assigned duties. See *accountability.*

**Rule.** A management-prescribed restriction or course of action.

**Scheduling.** The setting of times in the future when specific parts of a larger task should be completed.

**Span of control.** The scope of direct supervision over immediate subordinates. Usually the number of people under one supervisor.

**Staff employee.** One who is responsible for providing information, counsel, service, coordination (and sometimes control) to line employees.

**Standard.** A specific objective, the attainment of which can be measured or appraised.

## REVIEW

Name at least five elements common to all forms of management, from the oldest to the most recent.

What is your definition of "authoritarian management"?

What changes characterized the Industrial Revolution?

How does corporate ownership differ from family ownership of a company?

Name some techniques introduced by Taylor, Fayol and the Gilbreths.

What factors brought about a management accent on employee relations?

# 2

# STRUCTURING THE ORGANIZATION

A north Jersey chemist, out of a job in the Depression of the thirties, began concocting cleansers and polishes which he bottled in his basement. He put batches of filled bottles in the trunk of his car and peddled them to his friends and neighbors. This was a one-man business. The chemist performed the functions of purchasing his supplies, manufacturing his products, transporting them to market, selling them, and recording receipts and disbursements.

The business thrived. He hired a neighbor's son to do the production work. His wife took over the office work. The chemist continued to buy raw materials and sell the finished products. Ten years later he was managing an incorporated profitable business which employed 40 persons:

| | |
|---|---|
| 1 president (himself) | 2 maintenance men |
| 1 secretary | 1 shipping clerk |
| 1 vice president of manufacturing | 1 vice president of sales |
| 1 secretary and clerk | 1 secretary and clerk |
| 19 production workers | 3 salesmen |
| 1 production foreman | 1 treasurer; office manager, purchasing |
| 1 laboratory technician | 3 clerks |
| 1 quality control man | 1 janitor |
| 1 production scheduler | |

Most of these were line employees; a few were staff.

After 30 years of existence the company had 400 employees, 180 of whom would be classed as managerial or staff—quality control, production scheduling, industrial engineering, plant maintenance, costing, research and development, market research, advertising, sales promotion, clerical, accounting, electronic data processing, and long-range planning.

The organization chart continued to reveal a functional organization: purchasing, production, marketing, research, accounting and finance. Staff units were attached to line functions at various organization levels.

By the mid-sixties, the company was so strong financially that it could take a bold step forward: a second plant with sales offices on the West Coast. With this step, the company divided both the production and marketing functions on a geographic basis.

In the mid-seventies, the original entrepreneur turned over the reins to his two sons. One of their first steps was to build a highly automated plant for the sole production of industrial lubricants: product division in manufacturing.

The evolutionary growth of this profitable company illustrates the three basic organization patterns: functional, geographic divisional and product divisional.

## The Functional Organization

As a business grows beyond the scope and energy of one man, specialists are employed to supervise various activities. Perhaps the owner hires someone to supervise the production function. Later he may hire a manager to head up the sales function.

Figure 2a shows four functions only, but others will usually be found.

Characteristic of this type of organization, the executives in charge of the principal line and staff functions report directly to the president or to an executive vice president.

Organization growth consists of adding personnel to the basic skeleton. Occasionally an assistant or "assistant to" is designated to lighten the load on the head of the function. At lower levels foremen, subforemen, technicians, chief clerks, section heads, and branch

*Figure 2. Functional and divisional organizations.*

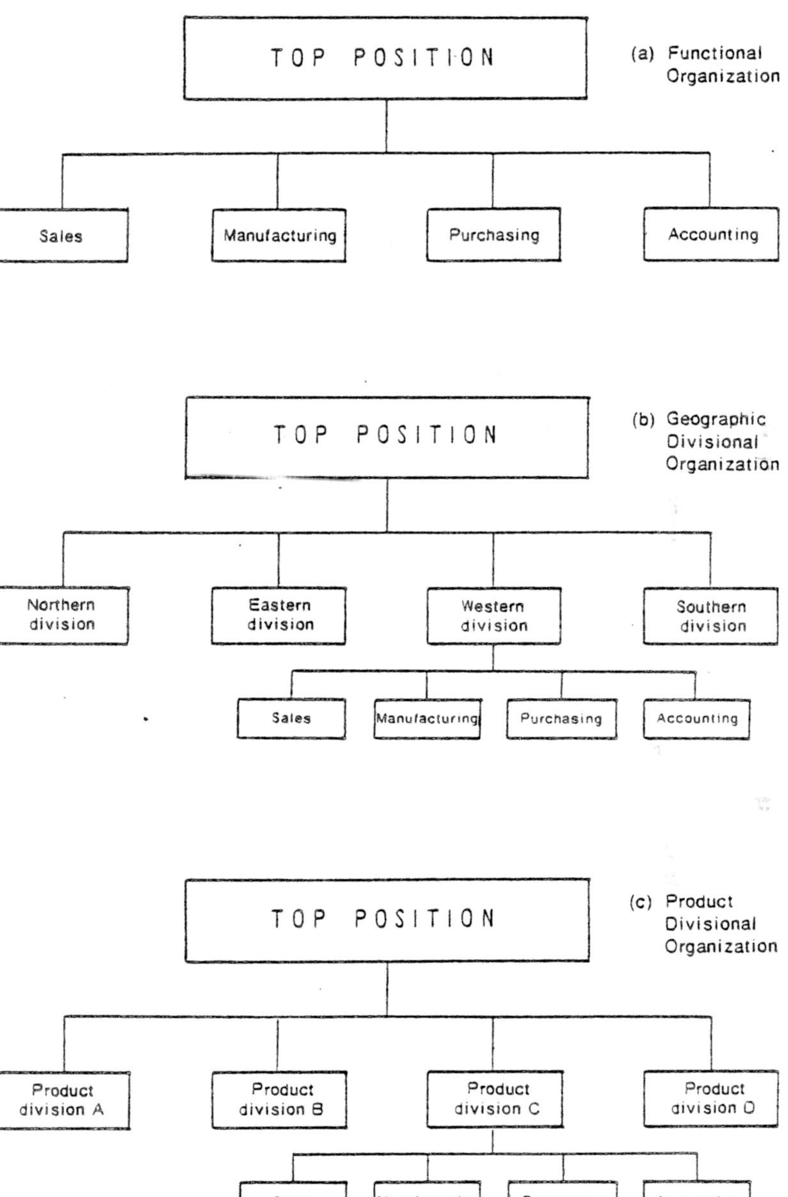

managers are appointed. These additions do not, however, change the basic functional structure.

## DIVISIONAL ORGANIZATIONS

If a company is widely dispersed, a geographic divisional organization may be indicated. Dispersion, or the desirability of dispersion, results from far-flung selling efforts, from widely scattered sources of raw materials, or from high costs of hauling raw materials or finished goods.

In one kind of divisional setup, branch plants are established at various geographic locations. In theory, each one is nearly autonomous as to manufacturing, selling, purchasing, accounting, and other activities. Figure 2b shows four geographic divisions, each of which has a functional organization.

Sometimes, all manufacturing is done at one plant location, but sales efforts are organized on a divisional, geographic basis. In this situation, top management needs to realize that policies and practices which operate well in manufacturing (probably for a functional organization) may not be applicable to marketing for a geographic divisional organization).

In some instances a company may manufacture such a wide variety of products, each with its own special requirements and problems, that it pays to set up special manufacturing units. In this event the organization pattern is likely to be that shown in Figure 2c. It reveals four *product* divisions, each one virtually autonomous as to manufacturing, selling, purchasing, accounting, and the like. Frequently a vice president heads up each division. Sometimes each product is handled by a subsidiary company with its own president and board of directors.

Often manufacturing can be done on a product divisional basis with a unified selling function organized on a geographic divisional basis.

Changing a manufacturing organization to either a product or geographic divisional basis (that is, branch plants) must be carefully planned because of the heavy plant investment involved and the upheaval to the existing organization. In any proposed reorganization the reporting lines and the authorities of staff departments or individuals present difficult problems for decision.

Many large organizations show a bewildering variety of organization patterns combined with confusing relationships of line to staff, and corporate staff to functional or to divisional staff. Unless responsibilities, authorities, and accountabilities are clearly spelled out, misunderstandings and conflicts are inevitable.

## Line/Staff Confusion

The words "line" and "staff" are used with so many different meanings that confusion results. They describe *relationships*—not departments or people, and sometimes not even jobs. Many jobs include both line and staff activities.

For example, a setup man in a machine shop produces nothing; he services a machine operator. Is he staff? A research and development chemist operates a pilot plant to produce a new product in quantities sufficient for sales department trial use. Is he line?

The confusion results from using the terms "line" or "staff" to designate whole jobs rather than certain types of activity. A given employee might wear both hats—the setup man might also operate a lathe, and the chemist might counsel operating people.

Here are two more definitions to supplement those in the Chapter 1 glossary:

*Line activities.* Actions directly involved in carrying out the primary functions of an organization.

*Staff activities.* Actions which provide information, counsel, service, coordination (and sometimes control) to line activities.

Several decades ago Peter Drucker, the well-known writer, teacher, and consultant, pointed out the emergence of "knowledge workers," distinct from blue collar and white collar employees. Many, but not all, knowledge workers are in staff positions. Theoretically they have little or no authority over line employees except the authority of knowledge. But line employees, supervisors, and even high level managers soon learn that it is risky to disregard the suggestions of seasoned knowledge workers. As a consequence, more and more decisions and direct orders come from them.

## Decentralized Profit Centers

Many managements try to place responsibility at decentralized profit centers such as geographic or product divisions. This idea is sound if the organization is geared to accept decentralized control. For example, top management must understand how to use accounting and budget reports submitted by the divisions. Also, the decentralized divisions, as profit centers, require capable managers who now think of themselves almost as if they were in business for themselves. If a company has previously been highly centralized, such entrepreneurial thinkers are hard to find among the division heads.

Setting up a decentralized profit center requires a lot of thought about the accounting concepts involved and, after it is in operation, requires considerable ability to analyze the findings. In some cases, for example in allocation of overhead, the center can be made profitable or unprofitable by a top level decision on cost allocation. A company with only one major product line should not attempt decentralized profit centers.

The typical decentralized control system makes the division manager responsible for earning a profit on the investment entrusted to him. Sometimes this runs the risk that he will take actions that are helpful to his division but are against the interests of the company as a whole. So the division manager must know what the company's best interests are and be able and willing to act accordingly. Sometimes the reverse is true. The program being adopted by the company as a whole is detrimental to the division and so invites opposition from the division manager.

The lesson to be learned is that much study and planning must occur before a decentralized profit control system can be successfully set up and operated.

## Organization Growing Pains

Top management must be able to recognize when the company is outgrowing its existing organization pattern. Here are 12 signs of growing pains. Having one or two signs may not be significant. But the presence of several almost certainly indicates the need for change.

*1. One or more organization levels between the first-line foremen and deciding authority.* The foreman asks for a decision from the assistant superintendent, who asks the plant manager. This situation can mean that the assistant superintendent hasn't been given sufficient power to decide or hasn't the courage to do so.

*2. A high level executive with various assistants and "assistants to."* This condition usually signifies centralization of authority in a situation where decentralization is needed. Generally, too many key men report directly to the top executive.

*3. Conflict between high level line and high level staff executives.* It takes careful analysis to distinguish which staff functions should be divisionalized, that is, which ones should be detached from headquarters staff and attached to divisional line executives.

*4. Conflict between corporate and division staff men.* Fault here may lie with the personalities of the men involved; with lack of understanding of authority, duties and accountability; with the reporting lines dictated by the organization chart.

*5. Shortage of executives.* Sometimes a company grows sales dollars faster than executives. Ill health, death, and resignations can cause shortages in managerial talent. Even when these conditions do not exist, a company may suffer executive shortage because the organization simply has not encouraged the development of executives. Usually such a company is the highly centralized, functional type.

*6. Methods are radically changed.* These may be in manufacturing, marketing, or administration and may involve new equipment as well as methods. Alteration of reporting lines may be indicated.

*7. Top level policies are altered.* These may apply in a number of directions: finance, ownership, production, marketing, products, labor relations, governmental relations, and so forth.

*8. Little lateral communication.* Functional lines are drawn so sharply that it is difficult for a middle management executive in one function to work with his peers in other functions; contacts between the two functions must be made through their respective chiefs. This bureaucratic situation often indicates empire building by high level executives.

*9. Too many committees.* Committees can be useful for information, participation, complaint drainage, or gathering of viewpoints.

But majority votes of committee members can rarely be substituted for a clean-cut executive decision.

*10. New plants, which are scattered geographically.* Geographic decentralization is likely to force authority decentralization. Until this occurs long-distance phone bills and long-distance frustrations are likely to be excessive.

*11. Product diversification.* The manufacture or sale of widely different products through existing production or marketing facilities may cause many growing pains.

*12. Competitors divisionalize.* When a competitor changes from a functional to a divisional organization, it's time to study changing, too.

Economists tell us that normal organization growth follows a cumulative S-shaped curve: a long period of struggling for existence, a rapid rise, a slowing to maturity. Some companies achieve their growth in 20 years, some in 50. Some never get off the ground. Management understanding of the need to change the organization pattern may release the growth hormone.

## RECENTRALIZATION

As previously noted, most companies develop as functional organizations. When either a geographic or product segmentation is introduced, decentralization has occurred only to the extent that authority has been delegated. With each decentralization, a counterpart control should be established at the source to insure accountability.

In some companies, factors are at work which lead to recentralization of authority. The main factors are:

*Top management disappointment over the results of decentralization.* Some divisional executives have failed to live up to expectations, perhaps due to insufficient experience, lack of conceptual ability, inadequate information, or narrow viewpoints toward profits.

*Introduction of electronic computers.* By centralizing the collection and interpretation of factual data, top management feels able to make important decisions better than hunch-following division managers. Similarly, operations research, with its application of complex mathematical concepts, must necessarily rest in the hands of a few staff advisers to high level management.

*Automation and numerical control.* Normally these features involve such radical changes in manufacturing and such large capital investments that decisions must be made at the top executive level or by the board of directors.

Neither centralization nor decentralization is in itself a good or bad thing. The probable effects must be studied.

## DIVISION OR SUBSIDIARY?

Extensive growth of a company may ultimately cause management to consider establishing a subsidiary company for manufacturing certain products, serving certain geographic areas, or servicing certain customers. Such a move involves problems in many areas:

Goals
Organization bylaws, authorities, policies, rules, and the like
Financing
Managerial capability for the proposed subsidiary
Compensation of its top officers and executives
Legal, including possible antitrust, implications
Accounting and tax (federal, state, etc.)
Competition and marketing
Accountabilities to the parent company and staff assistance from it

## A QUESTION OF GROWTH

In manufacturing, bigness of itself tends to cause growth. A large corporation with capable management can usually raise ample funds for added capital investment. Its incentives to do so may be:

Competition—domestic and foreign
Scarcity of skilled labor
Rising labor costs
Employee apathy toward quality
New products or markets
Availability of new materials
Changing consumer demand
Technological innovations—methods or equipment
Long-range plans
Management ambition

The nature of the industry has a bearing on growth. In a process industry such as petroleum refining, labor costs are low. A new large investment must be justified by an anticipated lower capital cost per unit of output. In the auto or radio industry where labor content is high, justification for growth may be reduced labor costs per unit of output or per dollar of sales.

Size may suffer penalties, also. Costly idle equipment can soon offset its hoped-for benefits. Although operating skills may be lessened, the need for maintenance skills may be increased. Small orders and short runs may not be economic; longer runs to handle accepted orders may result in unwanted inventory buildup. If the new equipment produces more, heavier, or more delicate products, then materials handling, storage, inspection, shipment, and transportation problems may become more complex.

The greatest challenge from enlarged capital investment will be in management itself. New organization relationships may be necessary for manufacturing, accounting, marketing, and staff personnel. There may be new problems of safety, pollution, legal standards, proper wage rates, or union opposition.

Despite the risks, most managers choose better equipment, which usually adds to existing capital investment. The decisions involved require use of sophisticated decision techniques. Some of these techniques will be considered in later chapters.

## Demand for Capital

An industrial society moves through a stage of standardization to one of diversification. The former produces identical parts and products at low cost. Varied consumer tastes, competition in the marketplace, new materials or technology contribute to diversification. Hundreds of products reveal this same evolution: foods, drugs, clothing, furniture, paper bags, soaps, magazines, automobiles, and others.

Advanced manufacturing equipment makes diversification feasible. The possibilities increase with computer (or even with tape) control of mechanical production equipment. The manufacture and purchase of such equipment requires an increase in capital investment.

Basically, capital results from wealth created by past production and not consumed. Manufacturing companies need working capital to meet payroll and other operating expenses. They also need invested capital to provide plant and equipment.

Worldwide industrializaion has created demands for more capital than is available. Additionally the capital needs of city, state, and federal governments are large. As a consequence, the demand for capital funds over the entire world exceeds the supply. The gap is filled by bank-created *credit*.

A corporation with less than an "A" credit rating will find it difficult to raise capital through issuance of bonds. Equity financing (selling common stock) presents other hazards. Too much borrowing loads a company with fixed interest charges, burdensome in periods of business recession. Too much stock issuance dilutes ownership and may reduce dividend payments thereby depressing the selling price of the common stock. A highly profitable company will try to satisfy its capital needs by "plowing back" a large portion of its annual net earnings. It will retain profits.

The whole subject of raising capital is beyond the scope of this book. The point is that it is an important and difficult responsibility for top management.

## Organization Theory

In recent years social scientists have developed a body of knowledge called "organization theory." It attempts to understand, explain, and predict human behavior when people are brought together into some form of organization. So far it is a loose agglomeration of findings and research methods from sociology, psychology, economics, and applied mathematics.

Organization theory has studied such subjects as leadership, morale, financing incentives, motivation, controls, freedom of action, small group behavior, communication, reactions to change, status, prestige, creativity, decision making, information systems, environment, and the effects of various kinds of organization relationships.

Some research devices which have been used in these studies have been:

- Observation of the behavior of people in groups by an outside observer or a participant observer.

- ☐ Controlled experiments, contrasting groups purposely subjected to different conditions.
- ☐ Development of mathematical models which include many variables that bear upon group behavior.
- ☐ Use of computers to determine the relative importance of each variable, or to predict the outcome if certain variables were to be radically changed.

Managers and prospective managers should keep in touch with developments in this important field of inquiry, which can serve as a basis for developing or improving one's managerial skills.

## REVIEW

Name four functions of a functional organization.

How is a divisional geographic company organized?

Name at least four growing pains of an expanding organization.

Name three ways for a company to get capital investment funds.

Name four or more subjects covered by organization theory.

# 3

# WHAT'S NEW IN ORGANIZATION CONCEPTS?

Nothing is certain but death and taxes—and changing management philosophy and practices.

At the turn of the century, railroads were the hot stocks of investors. None of their tycoon-managers would have believed that in 75 years their roads would be begging for government subsidies. For decades complacent railroad executives scorned the competitive threat of automobiles, buses, trucks, and airplanes. This is a classic example of the inability of some managements to adjust to change.

One writer, Dr. Laurence J. Peter, asserts that the pyramidal organization structure results in employees rising to their highest levels of incompetence. Employees who fail to do their jobs well will not be promoted but left at their present levels of incompetence. This condition he facetiously calls the "Peter principle."

## Weakness of Pyramidal Organization

Growth of corporations and scientific management have favored the hierarchical or pyramidal organization chart. Much of this concept was borrowed from military organization—line, staff, chain of command, span of control, to name a few terms.

The weakness of the orthodox chain of command can be illustrated by an episode in a large Southern cotton mill. A loom stopped because of a broken part, which could be easily replaced. The operator reported the break to the night-shift boss, who inspected the machine. He in turn wrote a brief report of the breakdown for the day-shift superintendent. The latter inspected the trouble and directed a machine-fixer to repair the loom. The fixer analyzed the problem and wrote out a requisition for the needed part, which the department foreman approved. The fixer then got the part from the supply room and repaired the loom, which by then had been idle for 15 production hours.

All the people involved in the incident, from the operator through the fixer, followed the strict chain of command of an organization chart. The system assumed that the loom operator was incapable of diagnosing the trouble, asking for the proper part, and putting it into place. It did not differentiate between a 30-second replacement of a machine part and a difficult mechanical repair job. Denied satisfaction by the system, the operator was outspoken in his resentment. "I could have fixed it in half a minute," he said. "As it was, I lost four hours' bonus."

Anyone who has drawn a typical organization chart has discovered that it imperfectly depicts relationships. Dotted lines are frequently used to denote partial, secondary, or indirect reporting to higher (sometimes peer) levels. Colored lines sometimes enhance the attractiveness, but not the clarity, of the chart.

The pyramidal structure is becoming less rigid. Authority is being diffused, some laterally but most of it downward. Centers of decision are spread wider and brought closer to practical operations. Control may be loose, but final results are stressed rather than intermediate activities. The whole trend is away from vertical administration and toward consultative operating relationships such as found in large consulting organizations or in research groups. If this relationship had existed in the cotton mill cited above, the loom operator would have removed the broken part, requisitioned the supply room for a replacement, and put it into place.

Multiple technology companies frequently bring together specialists from many disciplines to consider a complex problem. Some authorities refer to this approach as *matrix management*. It requires a detailed inventory of the specialized knowledge and skill of the persons available. A continuing management development program is essential for matrix management.

## The Matrix Organization

The matrix organization is built around contracts for large projects as distinct from normal production of goods and services. The aerospace industry is generally credited with its development although large engineering and construction firms have used it for many years without giving it a name. Figure 3 is a simplified illustration.

*Figure 3. Diagram of a matrix organization.*

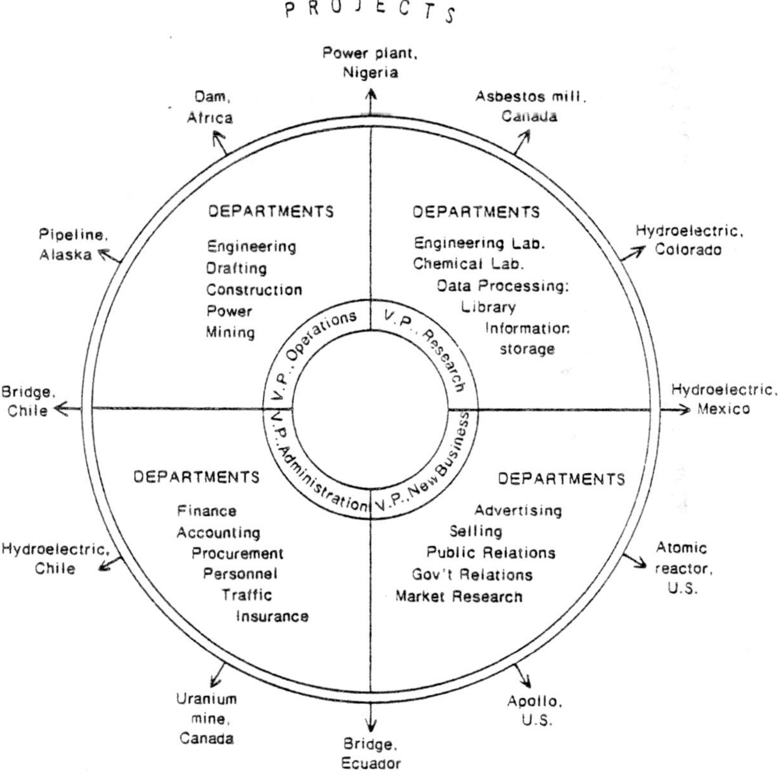

In a typical operation a project manager is assigned to carry out the contract. He plans all elements, probably preparing a PERT chart (see the next chapter). He borrows from the supporting organization the specialized personnel and facilities required to carry out his plan. Some personnel from the various departments may be needed for short assignments only; others may stay with the project from beginning to end.

For the duration of the project the manager (and his assistants) have complete responsibility. They have authority to hire, fire, order materials, subcontract, decide methods, determine standards of performance—in short, to get the project completed. At the end the project manager is accountable for quality, time performance, and profits. Personnel and facilities are then returned to the departments which supplied them.

Typically a matrix organization exists because there will be repeated, varied projects of considerable scope and duration. Orthodox types of organization, when faced with some special challenge, may set up a temporary task force with little disturbance to normal routines and organization structure. The distinction being drawn here is between a matrix *organization* and project management. The latter can be used in a pyramidal organization as well as in a matrix.

Managing a project team requires emphasis on certain aspects of management:

*The goal must be specific.* "To put a man on the moon" is a definite goal designed to motivate all participants. An objective "to increase corporate profits" would not be specific enough to provide comparable incentive.

*The selection of the team members is all-important.* They must be specialists in their respective fields, courageous in expressing themselves, cooperative with other members, and able to subordinate their opinions and ambitions to the common goal. Sometimes a team member with superior knowledge or experience becomes the actual leader of a project, despite the presence of an appointed leader.

*Since time is usually critical in a project, planning and control are important.* Gantt charts or CPM/PERT methods can serve both purposes.

*The project leader usually coordinates more than directs.* He must combine the knowledge and efforts of the specialists to achieve a whole which is greater than the sum of its parts. Nevertheless, when conflict or impasse arises or the program lags, he must be decisive and assert his authority. He will be judged by results, not by how well he planned, organized, coordinated, directed, or controlled.

*Throughout the project, the leader must maintain good relations with the managers of departments from which team members have been drawn.* Sometimes these managers interfere by giving orders to their loaned employees. Tact and firmness are needed by the project leader.

To some degree the behavioral sciences and the use of higher mathematics and computers have contributed to the use and development of project management and to the matrix form of organization.

## Executive Councils

The executive council is another type of organization which has evolved in very large corporations. For these companies the standard line and staff structure proved unwieldy, promoted empire building and internal conflict. In addition, heading up a giant company proved too difficult for one man as president. Some companies divided top executive responsibilities between the chairman of the board and the president—a move toward the executive council concept.

Figure 4 shows an executive council positioned between the president and the functional department managers. They consult with but do not report to members of the council. Each council vice president is responsible for his specialization *company-wide.* Thus the vice president of innovation might work with R&D, manufacturing, marketing, and cost accounting. He acts as a counselor and coordinator in much the same way as an outside consultant. The vice president of profitability could investigate any aspect of any department to improve company profitability.

Figure 4 also shows the use of teams (ad hoc or permanent) for performing *all* operations connected with a definite task or unit of output. Ad hoc teams have much in common with the task forces for completing temporary projects discussed under matrix management. Permanent teams will be discussed later in connection with job enrichment.

*Figure 4. Structure of an executive council.*

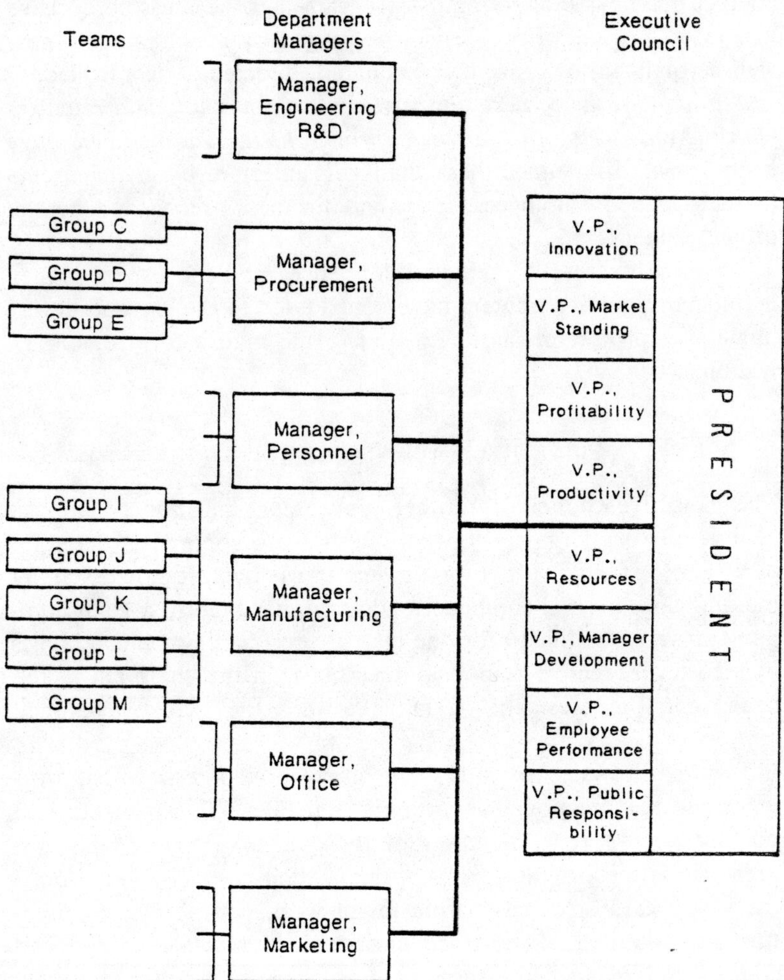


## THE PECKING ORDER

Simply stated, a pecking order is the sequence in which members of a group will accept direction from other members. Increasing use of consultative relationships and project teams may diminish but will not abolish the pecking order.

The authority of rank or of special knowledge will usually prevail. Trouble may occur when rank arbitrarily asserts its right to overrule special knowledge. But rank may, on the other hand, evade its decision-making responsibility by naively accepting the assertions of specialists. The ideal combination occurs when a ranking executive evaluates specialized knowledge pertinent to a clearly defined problem. He then makes a clear-cut decision in which he defines an attainable program of action which tells who is to do what and when.

## MILITARY-INDUSTRIAL ORGANIZATION

Huge sums spent by the military-industrial complex may be creating a variation of the industrial corporation. Companies receiving new large contracts for research or production take in a new partner, the federal government. The resulting military-industrial organization is far removed from the free enterprise system. As under fascism it is almost a captive of the state. Its organization may be either matrix or pyramidal and it may undertake extensive subcontracting.

Managers in such companies operate under legal, contractual, financial, and bureaucratic constraints not encountered by executives in normal market-oriented corporations. Excessive profits or losses may result in renegotiation of original contracts.

## THE INFORMAL ORGANIZATION

In every formal business organization there is a nebulous but real informal organization. Its key people may have little status. Its communication channels may be varied and unusual. Moreover, its standards of conduct are set by the group and may not be the same as the standards of the formal organization.

Here is an illustration of how the members of one informal organization, in a school system, communicated when the need arose: Whenever a teacher spotted a school district official parking his car, she would send children to other teachers with unwanted rulers, chalk, or other items. The alerted teachers would follow suit. Before the official was in the principal's office, every teacher had been forewarned.

Wise managers accept the existence of the informal organization and try to use it to accomplish worthwhile company objectives.

## Reshuffling the Organization

Reorganization is taking place continuously in every company. Deaths, resignations, incompetence, discharges, and transfers account for some of it. Other contributing factors are growth, product diversification, discontinuance of certain activities, new technology, new equipment, new methods, mergers, divestitures, and new ownership.

Sometimes only a single managerial job or a single department is affected. But if profits fall, a sweeping reorganization is likely.

Perhaps an outside consultant is brought in to make a comprehensive management audit. His recommendations are approved by the board of directors, but their implementation may take a year or two. A new organization chart is drawn, showing realignments of responsibilities, authorities, and accountabilities.

Fundamental to a reorganization is the management audit. A full-scale audit will question objectives and procedures in every area of a company. It will study interrelationships and recommend changes of financing, goals, methods, reporting, personnel, control and policies. In a limited audit, only certain activities will be subjected to close scrutiny.

An organization structure that has remained static for a number of years is probably geared to the past, not to the future. Planned change resulting from a management audit can prove self-renewing. All organizations should be continuously moving forward, not fixed.

## The Decline of Loyalty

Many forces are contributing to lower morale among executives, managers, and professional employees, as well as office and plant workers. One negative force is the decline of loyalty. A century ago, loyalty to an employer was taken for granted. Today employees flit from job to job, their increased mobility made possible by shortages of skilled labor and by the automobile.

Technical employees feel more loyalty to their respective sciences than to their employers. High level executives change jobs with increasing frequency for greater income, more challenging assignments, or greater future security. When key employees are moved around by their companies, they feel loyalty neither to any particular boss nor to the company which moved them.

Employee attitude surveys reveal lower morale and loyalty among employees who have stayed with one company for 10, 15, 20, or more years. This situation demands better leadership from managers. They should heed the words of some unknown savant who said, "Loyalty does not *well up* from the bottom; rather, it *trickles down* from the top."

## Economic Concentration

In this century three kinds of mergers have developed:

*Vertical integration:* buying sources of supply (backward integration) and marketing outlets (forward integration). For example, a paper manufacturer might buy a pulp plant and a paper converter.

*Horizontal growth*: buying up direct competitors.

*Conglomerate growth:* buying controlling interests in unrelated industries.

Acquisitions in foreign countries include all three types. Half of foreign acquisitions fail to prove profitable.

Each successful merger results in increased company size. The 200 largest U.S. corporations control almost 70 percent of the country's manufacturing assets.

Mergers cause numerous conflicts and changes in management practices: new reporting relationships, added controls, elimination of duplicate effort, standardization of procedures, and many others.

The merger alarm sounds repeatedly in Washington. Each new administration tries trust-busting. Size makes a company suspect, but current laws do not restrain "bigness" in itself and the government must fall back on charges of restraint of trade or of competition.

Social concern revolves around giant corporations' political clout, control over the lives of employees, or irresponsibility to ecological demands. Future managers must be responsive to these concerns.

## COMPUTERS: THREAT OR PROMISE?

In a few decades the computer has altered management as much as Taylorism did around the turn of the century. Under the impartial eye of the computer, mechanization has been changed over to automation. The end is not yet in sight. Additionally, vast amounts of almost instant information have been made available to management.

One of the biggest users of computers is the federal government: Social Security; Treasury, including Internal Revenue; Atomic Energy Commission; National Aeronautics and Space Administration; Veterans Bureau; armed services, to name a few users. Many local governments also use computers.

In the private sector, airlines, railroads, utilities, banks, insurance companies, and large manufacturing organizations have highly sophisticated computer installations. Even small and medium-size companies adapt electronic data processing to billing, payroll, inventory, accounts payable, and some research problems.

The computer threatens a new kind of bureaucracy accompanied by too much paperwork. Offices are becoming information factories. Except for the analysts and programmers, office employees serve the computers much like machine tenders in the factory. Some middle managers find that the computer has taken over much of their planning. Higher level executives look to computer printouts for help in making important decisions.

Furthermore, the computer has placed at various management levels a new class of mathematically oriented technicians. They have their own jargon and an approach to management problems different from old-line executives. They belong to the third grouping of employees: knowledge workers. Other knowledge workers include engineers and technicians needed for other highly sophisticated equipment.

Since the computer can quickly compile information on millions of people—personal data, credit standing, radical leanings, and much more—many concerned social thinkers fear that computers will lead to autocratic state control.

On the other hand, the promise of the computer is great. It is solving lengthy, complex problems. It can store voluminous data which are easily retrievable. Steam and electricity have freed human muscles of much of the drudgery that was their constant task. The computer can do the same for our minds, freeing them for creative thinking.

Properly used, computers will calculate the best uses of natural resources and will increase our understanding of the factors which make our economy tick. They may even help solve some of our sociological problems such as poverty, crime, racial tensions, traffic, and urban sprawl.

### The Unending Search for Efficiency

Throughout the ages man has sought better ways to get work done. The wheel is better than the sled, the steam engine better than the water wheel, the automobile better than the oxcart. Scientific management ushered in a methodical search for greater efficiency, a search which continues to this day. In other words, the object is to produce more goods and services with less labor.

Employee and consumer pressures have put the heat on management to raise wages and decrease prices, further stimulating the search for efficiency. Manufacturing, communications, and power utilities have probably been the sectors most successful in improving efficiency. The office, marketing functions, and agriculture have also responded well. Laggards in the search for efficiency have been construction, service industries, and various governmental operations.

## REVIEW

Sketch the organization chart of some company known to you.

What is project management?

If a company forms an executive council, why do department heads not report to it?

Recall some instance where you have witnessed the informal organization at work.

What benefits, and threats, do computers offer society?

# 4

# KEYS TO EFFECTIVE EXECUTIVE ACTION

Management in its administrative sense, can be broken down into five major divisions: planning, organizing, directing, coordinating, and controlling. Essentially these are the subdivisions first set forth by Henri Fayol in 1916.

Figure 5 shows the relationships between planning and the other four divisions. It also reveals that there can be relationships between each division and all others.

Planning and control are vital to effective executive action and are obviously related. There can be no control without planning. Too many times there is good planning with little or no control. Management planning and control exist in one form or another in every company. They are major management tasks.

## Planning

In the glossary in Chapter 1, "planning" was defined as "the process of determining goals and procedures; usually this means determining what, how, when, where and who." This definition includes the process of determining goals, policies, products, services, equipment,

*Figure 5. Relationships among the major subdivisions of administration.*

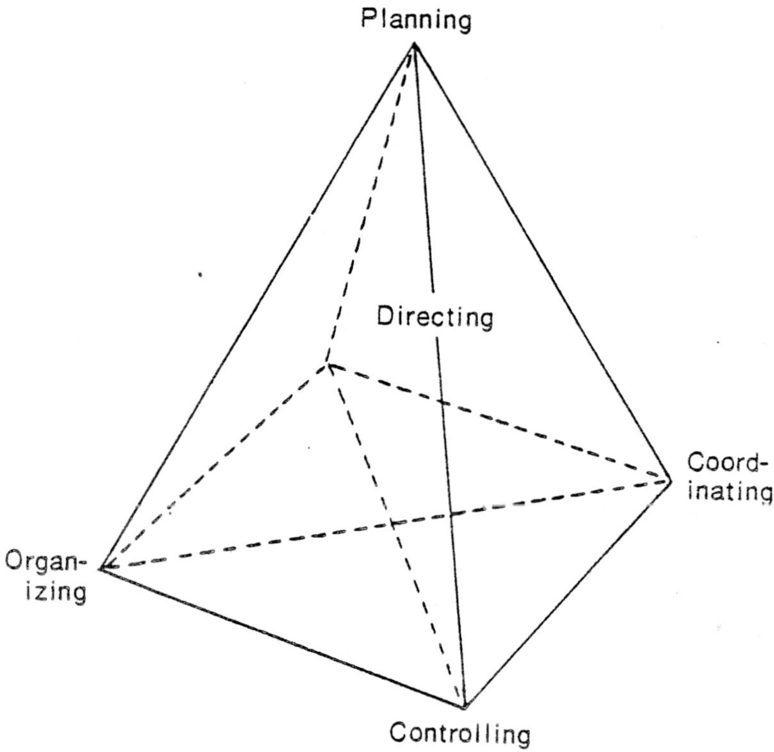


expenditures, procedures, schedules, locations, personnel, organization relationships, and related matters. Planning may have to be based on both fact and hunch. By increasing the number of relevant facts available, the use of hunch can be reduced, along with the planning errors that spring from it.

It is important to plan for retrenchment as well as expansion. Many companies add projects and personnel when profits are soaring but cut them out in a downturn. Retrenchment by giving up on a project is expediency, not planning. A program of planned economy will appraise present activities and assign priorities, so when cutbacks become necessary, completed market research, executive development plans, training programs, or new systems will not be haphazardly discarded. Nor will newly employed executive talent be cut simply on a last-in, first-out basis. The criterion for economy will have been carefully considered and planned. Unplanned cutbacks do not save money—they waste it.

Expense consciousness by employees and management achieves economies better than sporadic forays into cost cutting. A continuing program of economies with clear objectives can become as natural in operations as production or sales.

Most managements plan better than they control. To achieve balance, they do the following:

1. For each plan they determine its control and start controls at the same time as the plan.
2. They have a control for each function.
3. They establish controls which will cover the entire business, including return on investment, value added by manufacture, share of market, indices of growth, operating and financial ratios, cash flow and after-tax earnings.

Good managements make the manager of each function responsible for his share of the total plan and for planning the execution of that share by his own subordinates.

Short-range planning is a different problem from long-range planning. Both will be discussed here.

**Short-Range Planning**

Short-range planning includes periods up to one or two years and activities such as:

- ☐ Daily or weekly scheduling of production.
- ☐ Planning to move the office to new quarters.
- ☐ Getting a 90-day bank loan.
- ☐ Planning for sales calls on customers.
- ☐ Planning a special training program for supervisors.
- ☐ Constructing a new warehouse.
- ☐ Changing an inventory system from manual to computer.

Some short-range planning is merely a yearly subdivision of a long-range plan. Planning and implementation have largely been predetermined. The short-range task carries out a portion of the longer plan within a specified time.

A budget is an excellent example of short-range planning. Typically it attempts to forecast expenses for the coming year. It breaks down these expenses into various parts, such as labor, materials, and overhead. Since the budget often is based on a sales forecast, some companies set up a variable budget. In this they make two or three assumptions of sales, and hence production, and build an expense budget for each assumption. Normally the plan for job shop production is short, for mass production of a product is long, for mass production and assembly of standardized, interchangeable parts is longer, and for process production (as in petroleum refining) is longest.

### Long-Range Planning

This activity is very involved, and the treatment given here must be limited to an overview. Any comprehensive long-range plan considers every aspect of the business: organization structure, nature of jobs, qualifications of people, methods to be employed, equipment available, financing, public relations and other phases.

Before long-range planning, the company must make a basic decision whether it will make what it can sell or will sell what it can make. Each alternative points the company in a different direction.

Some companies consider their production capacity and forecast sales accordingly. This is a reasonable approach for companies which have decided that they will sell what they can make. However, if a company has decided to make what it can sell, the accent will be on market research, diversification, mergers, financial planning, or new technology. Such a company is not wedded to any one product or industry. It will make anything it can sell.

Long-range planning can be defined as a program of objectives and proposed actions covering a period of at least five years. Such planning must be based on certain assumptions, such as access to capital funds, energy available, technology developments still on the drawing board, long-term trends, the business cycle, economic wants, mass psychology, employee availability, competition, and legal restrictions. As the plan unfolds, it may be necessary to discard, add to, or alter some of the assumptions. Thus planning becomes continuous adjustment to an unknown future. Figure 6 shows that a company must look far beyond its own activities and resources to develop its long-range plan.

*Figure 6. Some outside factors in long-range planning.*

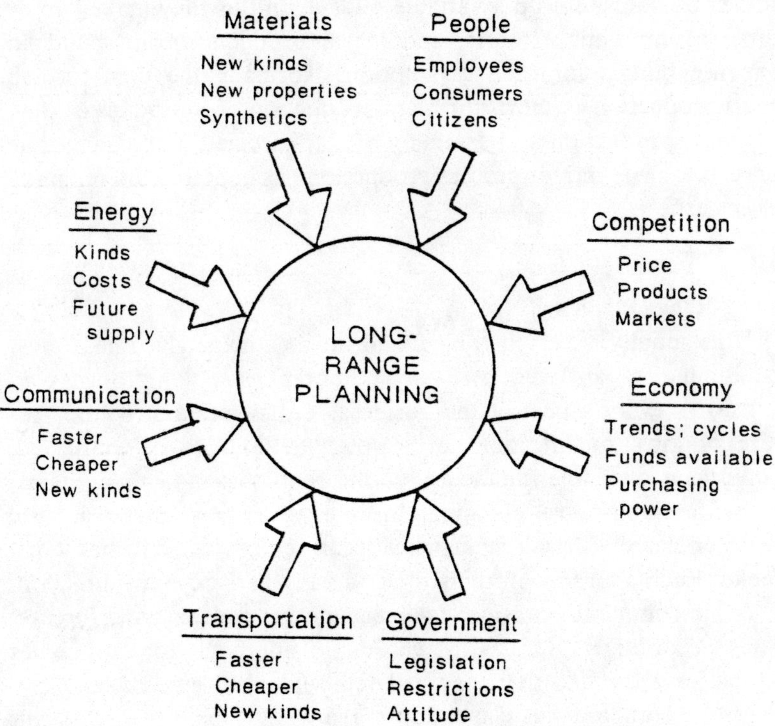


There are many factors which make long-range planning important. Companies are growing in size and complexity. They tie up large amounts of capital for long periods of time. Technological change has shortened the life span of new products. Investors expect quick returns. Increased education has raised people's levels of expectations and brought demands for higher standards of living and greater economic stability. Also, pressures have grown worldwide for state control of industrial production, multinational companies, and international competition.

Planning calls for action which may cause reactions that will necessitate further action. When planning, consider the *implications* of plans as well as the plans themselves.

*Figure 7. Simplified Gantt chart.*

**Shipments, On Hand and Unfilled Orders**

(Status Feb. 28)

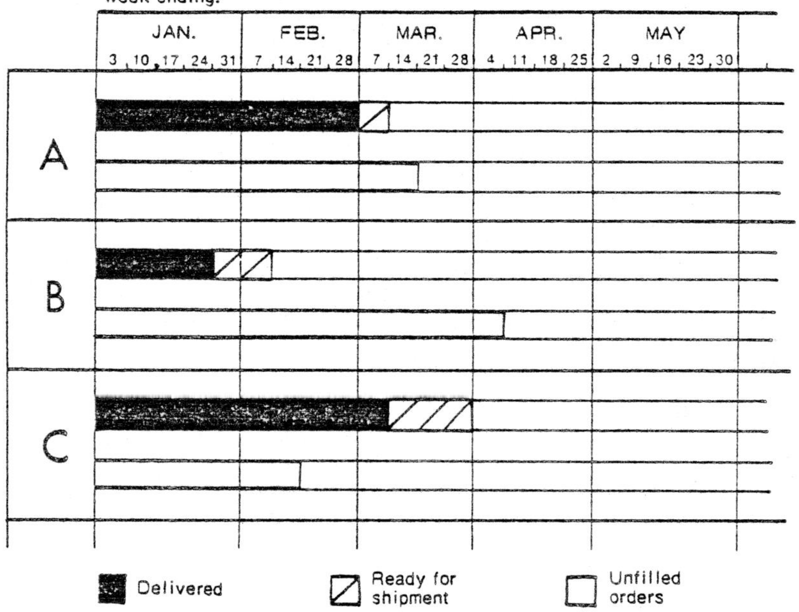


## TECHNIQUES IN PLANNING

There are some well-established techniques which can help in planning work. Some of these are graphic and some mathematical. The graphic techniques include Gantt charts, Plan-Trol charts, planning and scheduling boards, the Critical Path Method, PERT, and decision trees. Decision trees are covered in Chapter 10.

Gantt charts were devised by Henry L. Gantt, a management engineer. Figure 7 illustrates a portion of one type. At a glance it reveals that the deliveries of product B are in trouble. Charts of this type have found hundreds of applications—machine production, machine idleness, orders, purchasing, construction, employee output, installment payments, inventory, expense, sales, and many more.

The Gantt chart forecasts future events and measures actual progress against the forecast. It is a forerunner of the more sophisticated critical path network methods described in this chapter.

The Plan-Trol chart is based on a series of steps. These must be carried out by different persons at specified times so that the objective will be reached by the coordination of all their efforts. A Plan-Trol chart is shown as Figure 8. Its use follows a three-step sequence:

1. *Planning:* Break up the project into sequential steps. List these steps in the column headed "Brief statement of assignment" and number them in the first column. Show date *assigned* in the second column.

2. *Delegating:* Assign each item to one individual who will be responsible for its completion on time. Enter his name, date to be completed, and comments on procedures in the columns provided. Get each employee's agreement on the completion date. Be sure he understands what results are expected.

3. *Control:* This form provides control for the current month and the next two. Additional months can be added. Name the three months at the lower left. Next enter the assigned numbers in the proper calendar date follow-up spaces. Thus if the completion date for Item 1 is the twenty-fifth of the current month, enter "1" in the first space under 25.

Refer daily to the follow-up to recall what items should be completed. If they have been completed, cross out the item number in the follow-up section. Also place a check in the small box after the letters IC (item completed). If the work has not been done, advance the item number to some future date and cross out the current date. When items remain uncompleted, carry them forward to new sheets.

The Plan-Trol sheets can be kept in a three-ring binder. This simple technique of planning and control can easily be carried out by any manager.

### Planning and Scheduling Boards

There are many varieties of these boards. A simple one can be made by mounting several dozen hooks on a board. On these hooks, hang job tickets to show the various jobs which are flowing through a department. The tickets show expected completion dates.

*Figure 8. Plan-Trol chart.*

BENGE PLAN-TROL CHART
for executive planning and control

Enter here general subject covered by this sheet:

| Item No. | Date assigned | BRIEF STATEMENT OF ASSIGNMENT | Person assigned to | Date to be completed | COMMENTS – SPECIFIC INSTRUCTIONS, PROCEDURE, ALTERNATIVES, CONDITIONS, STANDARDS TO BE MET, AGREEMENTS, ETC. |
|---|---|---|---|---|---|
| | | | | I.C. | |
| | | | | I.C. | |
| | | | | I.C. | |
| | | | | I.C. | |
| | | | | I.C. | |
| | | | | I.C. | |
| | | | | I.C. | |
| | | | | I.C. | |
| | | | | I.C. | |
| | | | | I.C. | |
| | | | | I.C. | |
| | | | | I.C. | |

FOLLOW-UP

| MONTH | 1 | 2 | 3 | 4 | 5 | 6 | 7 | 8 | 10 | 11 | 12 | 13 | 14 | 15 | 16 | 17 | 18 | 19 | 20 | 21 | 22 | 23 | 24 | 25 | 26 | 27 | 28 | 29 | 30 | 31 | 32 |
|---|---|---|---|---|---|---|---|---|---|---|---|---|---|---|---|---|---|---|---|---|---|---|---|---|---|---|---|---|---|---|---|
| | | | | | | | | | | | | | | | | | | | | | | | | | | | | | | | |
| | | | | | | | | | | | | | | | | | | | | | | | | | | | | | | | |
| | | | | | | | | | | | | | | | | | | | | | | | | | | | | | | | |

As an example, in a central stenographic department, work may become lost or delayed unless there is some method of keeping track of who is doing what. By using a numbered job ticket for each assignment, the head of the stenographic department can determine the backlog of work, jobs in process, and which individuals are doing them. Job tickets of completed work can be used to summarize what has been done each day.

A more advanced form is the Produc-trol board. It can be applied to many work situations in addition to manufacturing. The standard board measures 3½ feet wide by 3 feet high and can accommodate 100 items. The progress of each item is recorded by a retractable cord which can be pegged on the board as work progresses. This is similar to a Gantt chart except that the retractable cord is substituted for the drawn line. The accent is on control of the preplanned work.

**Critical Path Method and PERT**

These are sophisticated techniques for planning and control. The Critical Path Method is often referred to as CPM, and the acronym PERT stands for "Program Evaluation and Review Technique." A number of variations have been developed, but all use a network diagram such as shown in Figure 9.

Critical Path *scheduling* involves arranging activities in sequence, diagraming them as in Figure 9, and estimating times for each activity to determine the minimum elapsed time for the whole job. CPM relates time for each activity to its cost, and determines whether times could be shortened by spending additional money. PERT, a similar system, works with high, medium, and low elapsed-time estimates, so allowing some latitude. Under these two systems, planning is at first separated from scheduling. This practice permits careful examination for the following purposes:

- ☐ To insure that activities are in proper sequence.
- ☐ To determine whether some activities can be done simultaneously with others to shorten the overall project time.
- ☐ To discover the *critical path* of activities, the total times of which will equal the anticipated overall project time.
- ☐ To note possible interrelationships or conflicts among apparently separate activities. Sometimes these relationships permit trade-offs

*Figure 9. Critical Path network.*

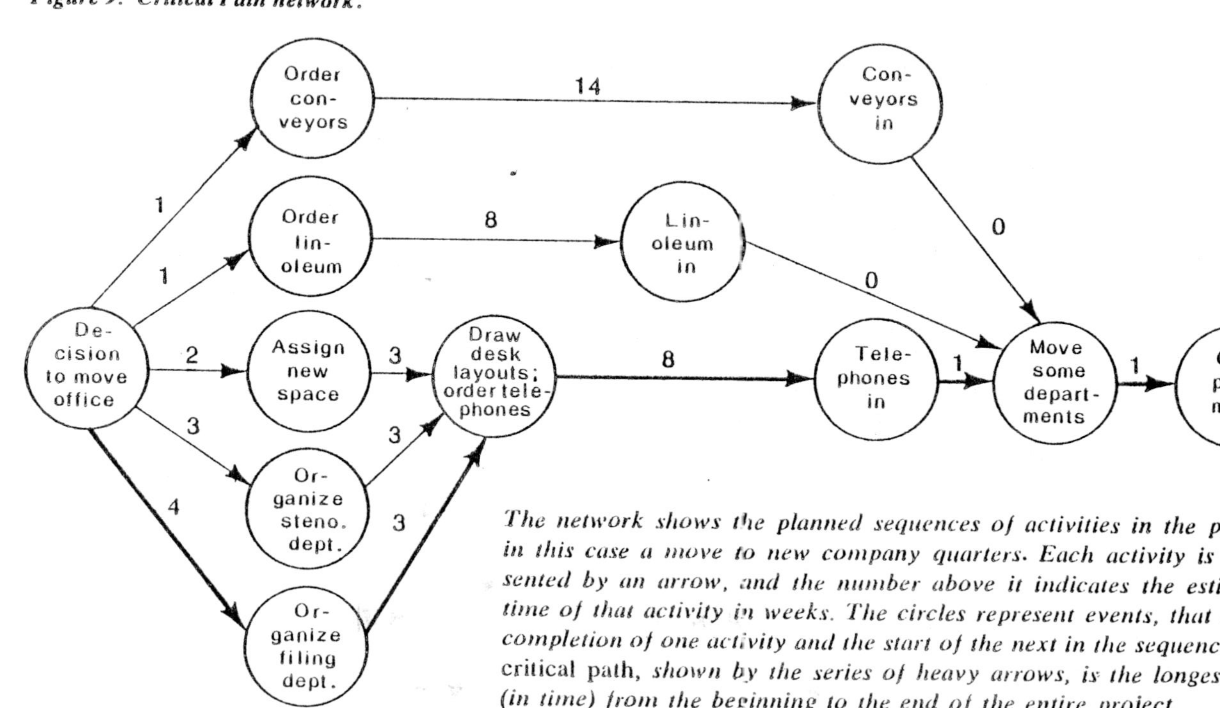


*The network shows the planned sequences of activities in the project, in this case a move to new company quarters. Each activity is represented by an arrow, and the number above it indicates the estimated time of that activity in weeks. The circles represent events, that is, the completion of one activity and the start of the next in the sequence. The* critical path, *shown by the series of heavy arrows, is the longest path (in time) from the beginning to the end of the entire project.*

of time, cost, personnel, or equipment to get a better balance of project elements.

- ☐ To examine all time elements before final schedules are set.

This book does not explain CPM or PERT in great detail. They are treated from the point of view of their values to modern management practice. Here are some values of network charting:

- ☐ It forces comprehensive and clear planning.
- ☐ It can evaluate alternatives and aid in replanning.
- ☐ It shows visually the scope of a complex project, sometimes highlighting missing elements.
- ☐ It clarifies who is responsible for doing what and when.
- ☐ It sets up a working model of the project to help key personnel see how their efforts will be integrated.
- ☐ It lays the foundation for managing the project by *exception*, which means that management intervenes only when activities fail to conform to the plan.
- ☐ It helps use labor and materials efficiently, lessens costs, and increases return on investment.

Computers have been programmed to use the Critical Path Method. This practice permits outputting weekly status reports.

**Mathematical Techniques**

Mathematics can play an important part in long-range planning but should not be used blindly to prescribe courses of action. Advanced mathematical methods help evaluate proposed courses of action and the influence of various factors. They can also give planners powerful tools for forecasting the future, even for exploring the implications of policies. Some planners are so enthusiastic about mathematical models, linear programming, and computer analysis that they accept the results without question. This is a risky substitution of mechanical methods for human judgment.

Many mathematical procedures are applicable to decision making and planning. One of the simplest of these is a projection of a time series such as annual sales using a curve on graph paper. Other factors being equal, projected future sales will continue much as in the past. Unfortunately, other factors are never equal. But the method does provide a base on which other influences can be superimposed. If growth has been irregular in past years, the average rate of growth can be used. But even this may not be applicable for future years. If the business cycle affects sales, the trend forecast must be modified up or down based on the direction of the current business cycle.

Another mathematical technique uses correlation combined with regression (prediction) techniques. This technique requires more training in statistical theory than is needed by merely projecting past history. Correlation measures the relationship between two variables and shows to what extent they vary against each other. Thus there might be a *negative* correlation between the Federal Reserve discount rate and the Dow Jones industrial stock index. That is, when one goes up, the other goes down. Conversely there might be a *positive* correlation between money supply and the Dow Jones industrial index: The market rises when money is plentiful.

Regression, built on correlation figures, weighs the importance of variables to predict an outcome. For example, wheat plantings, plus sunshine, plus rainfall might be used together to predict the wheat crop.

In addition, there are other sophisticated mathematical devices used in long-range planning, such as linear programming, mathematical models, and computations of probabilities.

Records, electronic computers, instrument readings, weather data, forecasts in other fields, impending legislation, monetary markets, international tensions, and the like, are also used in planning. Planning assumes that the future belongs to those who think about it.

## Control

Planning and control should go hand in hand. In fact, many of the techniques used in planning can become control devices. Wherever an executive has delegated authority, or a company has decentralized operations, there should be a corresponding control. Failure to install controls causes departments to move in so many different directions at once that profits suffer. Some top executives think of control as a method of directing lower level executives. That's not all there is to it. Control includes the means to appraise executive performance, to detect trouble spots, and to identify unprofitable trends.

Adequate controls using exception principles and standards can lighten the burdens of top executives. In practice, staff departments can operate controls and only report to top executives when situations get out of hand. Control is designed to find out if planning is carried out, to coordinate planning elements, to measure performance, to take corrective actions, and to provide information for future planning. Obviously such broad objectives must be made specific for each function of a business.

In situations where planning is based on time limits (as in scheduling, tickler files, Gantt or Plan-Trol charts or the Critical Path Method), the control is the passage of time. However, other controls may be based on quantity, costs, ratios, quality, payroll, or on opinions (as in employee attitude surveys).

In some situations, control is so far removed from specific planning, or is the combined result of so much planning, that it is difficult to establish a cause-and-effect relationship. Take, for example, profits per share, net worth per share, profits per sales dollar, return on investment, balance sheet ratios or break-even points. These indexes are the results of organization-wide efforts, not of some one specific plan.

Coordination can be a form of control. Coordination is the integration of space, time, energy, and material elements to provide unified action in carrying out a plan. Typically it is an intermediate form of control (as distinct from final control). Too much coordination results in red tape, friction, and killing initiative. Too little coordination results in chaos. Coordination usually requires daily or weekly supervision on the job, including, among other things, inspection, conference, coaching, and checking against schedules or standard costs. It should quickly put the spotlight on failure to comply, misunderstandings, friction, delays, commitments beyond authority, or other roadblocks to carrying out the plan.

Some executives prefer charts to keep track of past trends. Some, such as ratio charts, can be quite sophisticated and allow comparisons of dissimilar activities. Usually charts show progress against time as the base line, but they can also show correlation, regression, percentages, ratios, curves of first, second or third degrees, or other features which are part of the control method.

Increasingly, companies are setting up master control centers. Centers produce charts and data pertaining to costs, production, quality, markets, progress of long-range plans, employee relations, and social accountability. Centers may be the board room or a single office and may contain facilities for querying computers.

Reports to top management are common forms of control. To be effective, these reports should be timely, accurate, and standardized for quick reading by top executives. Standards should be included so the exception principle can be used to save management's time. Reports should give comparisons against a budget or previous periods. They should explain causes of unusual change or data. Tables, charts, conclusions, and recommendations are important elements in effective reports. When possible, they should predict the outlook for the near future.

Today management experts stress management by objectives or management by results. Actually, those concepts are dramatized versions of the subject matter covered in this chapter, namely, planning and control methods for managers.

## REVIEW

Name five subdivisions of administration.

How would you differentiate short-range from long-range planning?

Name three techniques of use in long-range planning.

Which two techniques use a network diagram?

Name some measurements used in control systems.

# 5

# OPTIMIZING HUMAN RESOURCES THROUGH SELECTION AND TRAINING

Setting policies for personnel selection and training is one of top management's top jobs. While top managers may not be directly involved in selection and training, except for their immediate subordinates, they bear final responsibility for the quality and effectiveness of company personnel. Their policy making affects the personnel department, the selection process, labor turnover, shortages of labor, employee training methods and developing key personnel.

## The Personnel Department

A fully organized personnel department will cover the following activities:

*Employment*. Application blank, interviewing, employment testing, explanation of fringe benefits, induction records, follow-up interview.

*Training*. Employee groups, apprenticeships, supervisors, key-personnel development programs, programmed instruction.

*Health*. Safety, working conditions, sanitation, eating facilities, conformity to laws, alcoholism, drugs, mental health.

*Employee relations*. Suggestions, complaints, rules and rule book, counseling, union relationships, minorities, collective bargaining, applications of fringe benefits, recreation, employee group activities, employee paper, communications, manpower planning.

*Research*. Personnel records, job descriptions, job evaluation, community wage surveys, performance appraisal, absenteeism, labor turnover, labor supply, labor legislation, validity of employment tests, personnel policies, employee attitude surveys, inventory of employee skills and interests, transfers, promotions.

How many employees should be there in the personnel department? All personnel functions are done somewhere in the organization by somebody. Quite often that somebody is an executive at a higher level than the personnel manager. How many activities will be assigned to the department? For example, is state compensation insurance, or employee insurance, to be handled in the personnel department or somewhere else? The same can be asked of training, safety, conformity to federal laws, and other areas of the company.

To assign as personnel manager an individual who has failed in some other position or one who is about ready for retirement is a grave mistake. The general attitude seems to be that anyone can manage the personnel function. This attitude will make a high-paid clerk of the personnel manager.

At the other extreme the personnel department may be loaded with specialists: psychologists, sensitivity training directors, working conditions inspectors, and executive developers. As a result of going to this other extreme, the personnel function becomes costly.

Additionally, some companies assign to the personnel department a telephone operator, a watchman, or a janitor. As a result there is a hodgepodge of activities dumped on the personnel function which diverts it from its true purpose.

As a rough rule of thumb, a company should appoint a full-time personnel manager when it has several hundred employees. Prior to that time, personnel activities are handled by an office manager, a purchasing agent, or supervisors.

When the work becomes too much for one person to handle, a typist and clerical assistant can be added. The personnel manager is freed for interviewing, conferences with foremen, and other personnel duties. Later an additional person may be hired for interviewing, safety, and perhaps training. Typically, this occurs when a company has between 300 and 400 employees.

In a multiplant organization there will usually be a corporate manager of industrial relations at corporate headquarters. At each plant there is some such setup as described above.

## Selection Is a Process

Selection of employees is a *process,* not a single act. Unfortunately, many companies pay more attention to buying a machine than hiring a person. This carelessness has been aggravated by skilled-labor shortages. The process of selection should include:

Job specifications covering the applicant qualifications desired.
Development of numerous sources of labor supply.
A preliminary interview of applicants to screen out the unqualified.
Completion of application blank by prospective employee.
Administration of *valid* employment tests when used.
Complete interview of those who pass the tests.
Former employment and references checked.
Interview by the supervisor involved, resulting in acceptance or rejection.
A physical examination for those accepted.
Written clarification of conditions of employment.
Introduction to fellow employees.

Employment managers may complain that this process is too lengthy; that applicants won't stand for it. However, competent applicants don't object to proving themselves by specific tests. Telephone contacts with former employers can speed the process.

For unskilled applicants the process can be shortened. But for others the time taken to hire competent, permanent employees is well spent.

## Labor Turnover

Labor turnover is one of the most frustrating problems management must face. In many companies the rate is over 50 percent annually. Much of the turnover occurs in the first few weeks of employment. Low level jobs might have to be filled a dozen times each year. So, a labor turnover percentage tells little about the stability of a work force.

To supplement the turnover index some companies calculate the average length of service. Other companies are interested in the percentages of employees in various service groups such as under one year, 1.0 to 4.9 years, 5.0 to 9.9 years, and so on.

Young and single employees change jobs more frequently than older and married workers.

High labor turnover is related to poor selection and inadequate training. Supervisors press employment interviewers to fill job vacancies. The interviewer refers poorly qualified applicants to the supervisors, who accept them. Within a few days or weeks new employees quit or are let go, and the dreary process is repeated.

To reduce labor turnover, the full selection process must be used. Then good job training, interesting work, and good supervision must follow.

## Skilled-Labor Shortages

Shortage of skilled labor poses another problem for managers. In some communities the problem is a shortage of any kind of labor, skilled or otherwise, which exists despite national unemployment statistics. Absenteeism compounds the problem, making it necessary to employ more people than otherwise required.

There is no single solution to the labor shortage problem. It must be attacked internally and externally. Following are some methods which companies have found helpful:

- ☐ Identifying the occupations in which shortages occur.
- ☐ Preparing a detailed job description of such jobs by interviewing present and former employees. This may bring to light conditions which can be corrected.
- ☐ Training employees in difficult job skills. This is the employer's responsibility. Some skills require much more training than others.
- ☐ Preparing employees for higher-skilled jobs while they are still on lower levels. Personnel records should be kept up to date and cross-indexed to show what skills are available. Companies with thousands of employees store such data for computer access.

- ☐ Studying employment records and tests to determine abilities and interests, which information can be used for transfers or promotions.
- ☐ Scouring the community for workers and not overlooking minority groups. Retirees can be re-employed. Women can be trained for jobs previously occupied by men. Part-time employees are a labor resource.
- ☐ Paying present employees bonuses for bringing in new employees who stay with the company for a specified period of time.
- ☐ Giving special attention to new employees during the start of their employment in order to slow labor turnover.
- ☐ Removing those negative psychological factors that cause employees to look for another connection in the first place. These will be discussed later in this book.
- ☐ Using job enrichment, discussed later, to stop the drain of employees, particularly at lower levels.
- ☐ Keeping employees informed of internal job evaluation and outside pay rates.
- ☐ Dividing high skill jobs into simpler parts so that they can be performed by persons of lower skills or training.
- ☐ Improving the company's image as an employer through public and community relations.
- ☐ Automating to reduce the need for skills for which labor is short. This requires capital and training technicians to operate the automated equipment.
- ☐ Using federal and state agencies which offer help to employers. Sometimes tax benefits are available for training persons receiving welfare.

## TRAINING

In many companies employing fewer than a thousand persons, organized employee training is a forgotten art. Some employers feel that training is wasted. It causes employees to seek jobs elsewhere or invites other employers to lure trained people away. This kind of management thinking contributes to shortages of trained labor.

As stated earlier, careful selection of employees is important to insure competence. Further, it is easier to train a well-selected employee than one poorly selected.

There are dozens of audiovisual and other training aids available to any employer for formal training programs. These aids include slides, overhead projectors, sound-slide and filmstrip projectors, motion pictures, video cassettes and cartridges, long-playing records, duplicating machines, tone-type telephone remote control of audiovisual presentations, instructional headphones for individual listening, video tape players, flip-chart pads, flannel boards, magnetic boards, bulletin boards, chalk boards, cork boards, public-address systems, lecterns, teleprompters, programmed instruction machines or books. Audiovisual training is superior to lectures alone.

Aside from equipment there are video tape lease libraries, workshops to instruct training directors in the use of audiovisual equipment, catalogs and directories, recorded courses of instruction. Several magazines are devoted to the audiovisual field.

*Programmed instruction* (PI) involves analysis of the material to be learned and arrangement of its presentation to proceed from the known to the unknown and from the simple to the complex.

Sometimes the presentation is in book form. Explanations are given and questions asked on each phase before the learner moves on to the next phase. PI gives immediate reinforcement of learning.

A highly sophisticated method of programmed instruction uses a computer which tells the learner if he is right or wrong. If the learner gives an incorrect answer, the computer provides an additional bit of information or tells him where to review before going ahead.

The *job-instruction training* (JIT) method has proved very successful for breaking in production workers. It is built around four rules: (1) Tell the learner; (2) show him; (3) have him do it; and (4) check that he does it properly.

Group training of knowledge workers can be done by the *discussion* method. Using this method, the conference leader poses a problem, then asks for ideas from participants. He lists the suggestions in brief on a blackboard, classifying them under logical headings. Finally the group sees one or more solutions to the problem under discussion. A case study can be used as the problem, in which event participants are usually given the details of the case in advance.

*Repetitive impact* training is useful for developing manual skills. The skill is first analyzed for the best sequence of operations. Next, a motion picture is made of the particularly difficult operations as performed by a skilled worker. The film is made into a single loop so that it can be run continuously. At first it is run in slow motion to enable the learner to imitate the movements of the skilled worker. The film is then gradually speeded up until the trainee can perform the difficult operations rapidly, with no skill hazards. This is the repetitive-impact aspect of the training.

In a highly decentralized organization, such as the Union Carbide Corporation, a *printed manual* may serve the dual purpose of training and standardizing procedures. UCC, with 95 field purchasing locations, has issued a training and reference guide that uses the UCC *Purchasing Policies and Procedures Manual* "as the basic text." The *Workbook* is supplemented by an *Instructor's Guide,* various visual aids, and case studies.

UCC reports that the *Workbook* has been "extremely effective." Imagine the chaos in a company of this size without such carefully planned manuals to control purchasing practices.

## Development of Key Personnel

Every organization has key positions, such as executives, department managers, foremen, staff specialists, and technicians. Many have experience in one area only but find themselves wrestling with human relations or other problems for which they have little competence.

This situation has brought about foremen training, executive development programs, and various methods of developing key personnel. Foremen training has been used for many years. Critics say that it has informed foremen without producing much change in their supervisory practices: They were trained but not developed. Supporters believe that modern approaches, including the techniques presented in this chapter, are improving supervisory attitudes and practices, especially since more supervisory jobs are held by younger and better-educated persons.

Most companies have a few employees with undiscovered talent—diamonds-in-the-rough needing to be polished. However, since there are so few of such employees and since competition for key managers is increasing, there is a need for a strategic approach to manpower development. A company can buy materials, hire labor, and rent capital, but it must find and develop managers. When it loses a key manager, it loses the thousands of dollars invested in him and must start all over again.

Key-personnel and executive-development programs have been more than training. Selected candidates have been sent to workshops, seminars, and courses conducted by universities, professional associations, or consultants. Many companies internally train executives and key people.

Development goes beyond training. It requires changes in attitudes, working habits, and personal traits and in learning, problem solving, and decision making. As development tools, companies have used psychological tests, tests of interest, performance appraisals, counseling interviews, special research assignments, job rotation, special project assignments, leaves of absence for political and social work, foreign assignments, and management of branch plants or subsidiary companies. Many of these approaches develop through challenge. They represent thousands of dollars' investment in individuals who are thought to possess great potential.

The secret of the success of General Motors Corporation, which has solved problems caused by its great size, lies in developing managerial talent at all levels. In fact, such development is considered a prime responsibility of each manager. In 1921, General Motors suffered a deficit of $38 million. When Alfred P. Sloan became president, he instituted a change in company philosophy which soon reversed GM's losses and converted it into the largest manufacturer in the world. His program included manager development at all levels. Sloan wrote:

> Place in charge of each part the most capable executive that can be found, developing a system of coordination so that each part may strengthen and support each other part, developing ability and initiative through the instrumentality of responsibility and ambition—developing men and giving them an opportunity to exercise their talents, both in their own interests as well as those of the business.

To implement this philosophy, the company prepared for its major executives an Advanced Management course which included comprehensive readings on economics and other social sciences. Managers at various levels participated in free-discussion meetings to review policies and problems. Informality prevailed, with little attention given to title or rank. A manager's effectiveness was in part judged on how well he had developed subordinate managers. Peter F. Drucker, who made an intensive study of General Motors, wrote in his outstanding book *The Practice of Management,* ". . . no one develops as much as the man who is trying to help others to develop themselves."

Some large corporations consider the problem of key-personnel development so important that they have established "assessment centers." The center brings together a team of trained observers who make assessments of selected candidates for promotion as they participate in various developmental exercises.

Not all key-personnel development programs have been successful. Some of the causes of failure are listed at the top of the next page.

In developing individuals who have potential, there really is no substitute for challenge. By position rotation a manager can soon find a candidate who is worthy of new challenges. These actions must, of course, be supplemented by additional knowledge and skills.

In breaking in a new manager, top management has five choices of action:

1. Throw the full weight of the new assignment on him.
2. Give him several weeks of intensive orientation.
3. Have him work with the former position holder until he has mastered all details.
4. Have other executives who relate to his new job explain their responsibilities to him.
5. Gradually increase the responsibilities of his new job.

In practice, combinations of these choices will usually be used.

To date, the training of future managers has followed the procedures outlined in this chapter. In recent years some new features have been added. Sociology, cybernetics, theory of statistics, com-

1. Management

No organization goals set.
No top-management support.
Failure to involve managers.
No organized program stating what, how, when, by whom.
No funds budgeted for program.
No control of costs.
Bad organization climate.
Hostility from a candidate's boss.
Inadequate communication of program and its objectives.
No deadlines set.
No periodic checkup of results.

2. The Candidate

No analysis of his background: childhood, education, experience, age, physical condition, etc.
No analysis of his job performance, personal traits, emotional adjustment, attitudes, ambitions, motivations.
No aptitude testing of abilities and interests.

3. The Program

Too much dependence on printed information or lectures.
Too academic; over the candidates' heads.
Sole reliance on outside training.
Poor publicity.
No verbal encouragement from top.
No financial or opportunity incentive.
No promotions traceable to the program.
No opportunity to practice new knowledge, skills, or viewpoints, or to make decisions.
No transfers for experience.
Lack of performance standards, challenge, competition, or broader contacts.

4. The Program Manager

Status too low.
Inadequate knowledge.
Poor personal traits.
Fails to lead.

puters, information systems, consumer motivation, unionism, public relations, and long-range planning are examples of subjects being included in management training. Executives are being loaned to government and educational institutions for experience and for mutual understanding of each other's problems. Temporary assignments to project teams increase versatility and provide experience in consultative management. In such assignments, rank is often ignored, conformity is not a virtue, and creativity and experimentation are encouraged.

With the benefit of these expanded horizons, the manager of the future is bound to be a person of broad vision and many talents.

## REVIEW

Name ten important activities of a large personnel department.

A company employing 400 persons loses 20 of them in a month. What is the annual percentage turnover rate?

Name five things an employer should do when faced with labor shortages.

Name six audiovisual training devices.

What is the difference between training and development?

Give six possible reasons for failure of key-personnel development programs.

# 6

# PAYING PEOPLE FOR PURPOSE AND PROFIT

Money isn't everything. Nor are fringe benefits. Many people of the Vietnam generation have practiced a life-style which makes money seem less important than it was to their parents.

Yet, compensation and fringe benefits still occupy a central role in all economic systems. Within companies, they take up a great deal of management's time. No management decisions have more lasting impact on the success of a company than those which affect the paychecks of employees, from the president's to the lowest clerk's.

## Compensation Methods

One time-honored compensation method pays employees by the hour, the day, the week, or the month. Time is easily measured, making payroll computations relatively simple. However, while this method makes labor costs easy to estimate, it provides little incentive.

Another long-used system is the piece rate, in which employees are paid for producing units. The price paid for each unit is set in advance so that labor costs per unit will be fixed. The employee knows in advance what the per unit price, or piece rate, is. This plan provides considerable incentive to capable employees, but it results in inequities in earnings when piece rates have not been set properly in relation to one another. Suppose it takes skilled workers like Tom and Bill the same amount of time to produce either a widget or a whatsit. But in their company the piece rate is 10 cents higher for a whatsit than for a widget. This means that Tom, who is working on widgets, is getting paid less than Bill, who works on whatsits, even though Tom works as fast as Bill.

Scientific management, using time study, set standard times for certain tasks and offered incentive bonuses to workers who produced more in the allotted time. Differential piece rates and premium systems were also developed.

Time study had ready application to repetitive jobs. But many plant and office jobs continued under payment for time. Even time study, which yielded expected units of production per hour, needed an hourly rate to translate time to money. Also, what per cent bonus on what hourly rate should be paid a worker for meeting standard time?

Plantwide incentive systems have been developed whereby employees and supervisors share in a bonus if the entire plant reaches an agreed-upon standard. This approach is similar to profit sharing. Under profit sharing a percentage of profits is allotted to participants by means of a distribution formula. Frequently, a more generous formula applies to executives.

Stock purchase plans are another compensation benefit for executives and managers. Some stock purchase plans include a matching contribution by the company. Other companies offer stock options, in which key employees can purchase company stock at a fixed figure. For option plans qualified with the Internal Revenue Service, the price must be 100 percent of the market price on the date the option is granted. Holding periods and other rules also apply.

## Job Evaluation

Job evaluation helps determine hourly rates for nonincentive jobs and base hourly rates for incentive jobs. The main factors bearing on compensation questions are:

- ☐ The work itself: duties, responsibilities, requirements, and working conditions. Job evaluation covers this area.
- ☐ Economic conditions: inflation or depression, labor scarcities, competitive labor rates.
- ☐ Industry practices.
- ☐ The company: policies, profitability, fringe benefits.
- ☐ The worker: attitude and performance.

A complete program of wage and salary administration will include job evaluation, a survey of local wage rates and personnel practices, application of knowledge of industry practices, application of company policies, and performance rating of employees.

Unfortunately, job evaluation came into general use some decades after time study. By that time, about 1940, piece rates and other incentive pay plans had resulted in inequities in employee earnings. In fact, some companies undertook job evaluation to help correct incentive pay earnings.

Over the years four systems of job evaluation have been tried:

1. Job ranking, usually done by a committee of informed persons.
2. Predetermined grades, which are first defined by education, experience, skill, and other requirements. Jobs are then assigned to grades by a committee.
3. Point systems, described below.
4. The factor comparison system, described below.

The simple procedures of the first two have been merged into the other two.

**Job Evaluation by the Point System**

Under the point system certain factors are designated by which jobs will be evaluated. A widely used plan of the National Metal Trades Association is based on the following 11 factors: (1) education required, (2) experience required, (3) initiative and ingenuity required, (4) physical demands, (5) mental or visual demands, (6) responsibility for equipment or process, (7) responsibility for material or product, (8) responsibility for safety of others, (9) responsibility for work of others, (10) working conditions, and (11) unavoidable hazards.

Each of these factors has five degrees. Points are allowed for each degree. Thus the five degrees of education may be allotted 14,

28, 42, 56, and 70 points respectively. Experience degrees may be allotted 22, 44, 66, 88, and 110 points.

Job descriptions are prepared, and a committee allocates the proper number of points for each factor. In this way a total number of points is reached for each job. These points are then converted to money.

In practice the points are assigned to job levels or grades. Each grade has a "min" and a "max" of both points and money values. By this method any job can be assigned to its proper grade. Typically the money spread in one grade is 30 to 40 percent, max over min.

The point system is easily compiled and easily understood, so it appeals to the sense of fairness of most supervisors and employees. However, it has some disadvantages:

- ☐ It uses a fixed number of factors (in our example above, 11) to describe every job.
- ☐ The assignment of maximum point values for each factor is arbitrary. A comparison of point plans, company to company, often shows different maximum point values assigned to factors such as skill or experience.
- ☐ Points are not defined. Is a point of education equal to a point of experience or a point of responsibility? Also, too often the person writing the job description, rather than a committee, sets the point values. If in the job analyst's opinion the job requires a high school education, the number of points for the educational requirements of that job has been set arbitrarily.

### Job Evaluation by the Factor Comparison System

The factor comparison method overcomes some of the weaknesses of the point system. It uses five factors: (1) mental requirements, (2) skill requirements, (3) physical requirements, (4) responsibilities, and (5) working conditions.

As under the point system, job specifications are prepared and divided among the factors. However, the factor comparison system creates a *key scale* for measuring jobs. This is the basic difference between it and the point system. Figure 10 illustrates a key scale. Normally 20 or 30 typical jobs in the company are analyzed to form the key comparison scale. The scale is expressed in units rather than points, and the units are a function of money.

*Figure 10. Typical key scale.*

| UNITS | MENTAL FACTOR | SKILL FACTOR | PHYSICAL FACTOR | RESPONSIBILITY FACTOR | SUPERVISION FACTOR | UNITS |
|---|---|---|---|---|---|---|
| 87 | | | | | | 87 |
| 86 | | | | | Mgr. Coll. & Ex. M-1 | 86 |
| 85 | | | | | Purchase Agt. P-1 | 85 |
| 84 | Mgr. Coll. & Ex. M-1 | | | | | 84 |
| 83 | | | | Savgs. Tel. S-1 | | 83 |
| 82 | | Mgr. Coll. & Ex. M-1 | | Coll. Cust. C-1 | | 82 |
| 81 | Coml. Teller C-5 | | | | | 81 |
| 80 | Purchas. Agt. P-1 | | | | | 80 |
| 79 | Coll. Cust. C-1 | | | | | 79 |
| 78 | Bookkpr. Tr. B-1 | | | | | 78 |
| 77 | | | | | | 77 |
| 76 | | | | | | 76 |
| 75 | | | | | | 75 |
| 74 | | | | | | 74 |
| 73 | | | | | | 73 |
| 72 | | Coml. Teller C-5 | | | | 72 |
| 71 | | Genl. Auditors G-1 | | | | 71 |
| 70 | | Bookkpr. Tr. B-1 | | | | 70 |
| 69 | | Savgs. Teller S-1 | | | | 69 |
| 68 | | | | | | 68 |
| 67 | | Addressograph A-2 | | Mgr. Coll. & Ex. M-1 | | 67 |
| 66 | | Coll. Cust. C-1 | | | | 66 |
| 65 | | | | | | 65 |
| 64 | | | | | | 64 |
| 63 | | | Coml. Teller C-5 | | | 63 |
| 62 | | | Messenger Ml. M-2 | Genl. Auditors G-1 | | 62 |
| 61 | | | Savgs. Teller S-1 | | | 61 |
| 60 | | Typists Clk. Br. T-2 | Bookkpr. Tr. B-1 | | | 60 |
| 59 | | File Clerk F-1 | Addressograph A-2 | Typists Clk. Br. T-2 | | 59 |
| 58 | | | File Clerk F-1 | Messenger Ml. M-2 | | 58 |
| 57 | Steno. Clerk S-4 | | | Steno. Clerk S-4 | | 57 |
| 56 | | | Mgr. Coll. & Ex. M-1 | Bookkpr. Tr. B-1 | | 56 |
| 55 | Typists Clk. Br. T-2 | | | | | 55 |
| 54 | Savgs. Teller S-1 | | | | | 54 |
| 53 | Messenger Ml. M-2 | | | | | 53 |
| 52 | | | | | | 52 |
| 51 | Addressograph A-2 | | | File Clerk F-1 | | 51 |
| 50 | File Clerk F-1 | | Genl. Auditors G-1 | | | 50 |
| 49 | | | Acctg. & Taxes A-1 | | Genl. Auditors G-1 | 49 |
| 48 | | | Asst. Bldg. Mgr. A-3 | | | 48 |
| 47 | | | Steno. Clerk S-4 | | Acctg. & Taxes A-1 | 47 |
| 46 | | Messenger Ml M-2 | | | Bookkpr. Tr. B-1 | 46 |
| 45 | | | Coll. Cust. C-1 | | | 45 |
| 44 | | | | | | 44 |
| 43 | | | | | Coll. Cust. C-1 | 43 |

Using job specifications, a committee compares each job against the scale, *one factor at a time*. In essence, by positioning the job in relation to other jobs, the committee determines the number of units to be assigned to it. The total units represent the total value of the job, and they are translated into money by means of a scatter diagram (see Figure 11).

The factor comparison system recognizes that as jobs of higher levels are included, the nature of the five factors may change.

*Figure 11. Scatter diagram.*

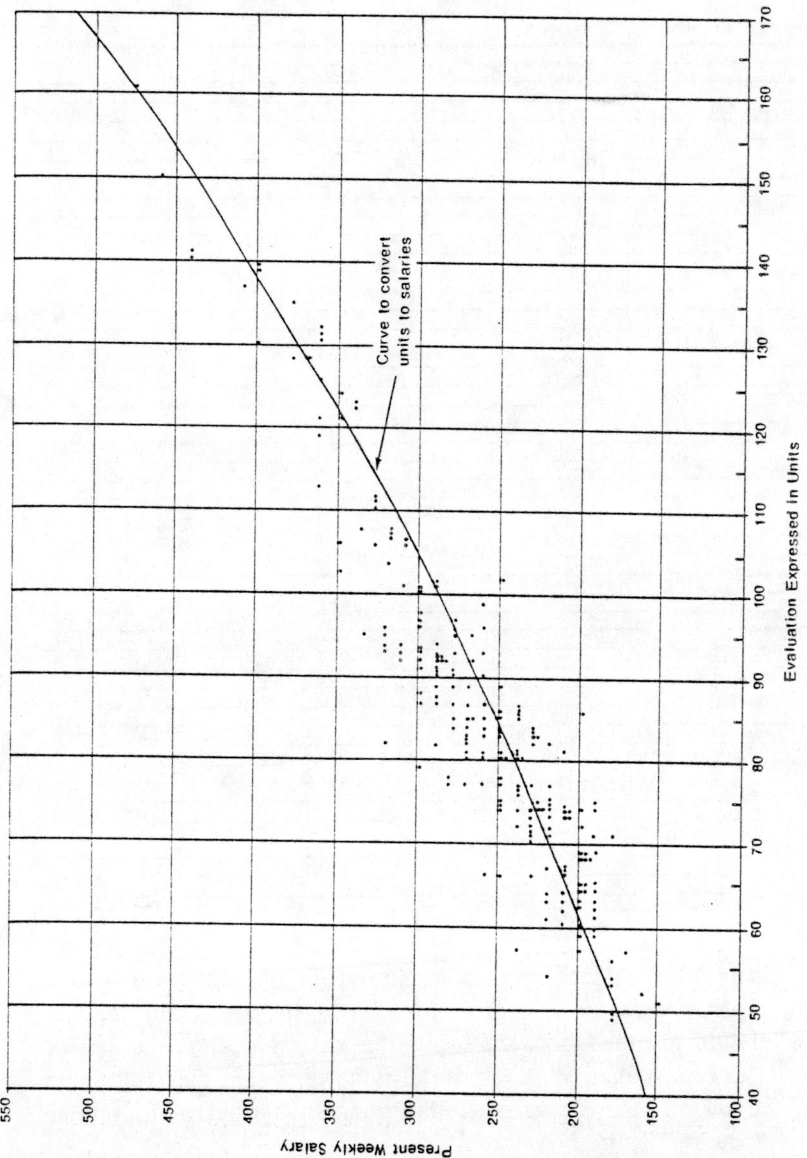


Physical requirements may lessen considerably, and skill requirements may change from manual dexterity to supervisory or conceptual skill. Furthermore, the mental demands and responsibilities may increase radically.

Since there is no ceiling on the number of units which can be assigned, it's possible to add higher levels of jobs to an original system. This is an advantage over the point system, which requires setting up separate systems to take care of technical, supervisory, and managerial tasks.

The point system of job evaluation is easier to develop, apply, and explain than the factor comparison system, but it breaks down more easily under employee or supervisory pressure. The factor comparison system works better for office, technical, and supervisory personnel.

Since both systems assign jobs to grades, with min and max pay rates, some method is needed to determine when present employees should receive pay increases within their grade limits. Performance appraisal meets this need in an organized way.

## Performance Appraisal

The early methods of evaluating employee performance were known as "merit rating plans." Most of them fell into disrepute. Their principal weakness came from rating *personal* traits only—such as dependability, potentiality, and versatility—while ignoring quality and quantity of work. Eventually it was realized that the evaluation of employees should be based primarily on *performance*. In addition, some traits, such as the following, are included: "Offers suggestions," "accepts added responsibility," "shows ingenuity," "continues to learn," "is highly skilled," "meets deadlines," "is physically energetic," "cooperates with others."

From scores of such items, ten traits which are pertinent to almost any job can be selected. Add ten job specifics and these 20 become the items for appraising performance. The items will not be the same for all jobs, although supervisory jobs usually have the following in common: "trains employees," "issues clear instructions," "builds employee morale," "is careful about safety," "uses equipment properly," "reduces costs," "operates within the budget," "seeks better methods," "develops performance standards," "plans work," "increases productivity," "prepares good reports," "controls work of subordinates," "cooperates with his superior," "carries out company policies."

Each pertinent item can be given the point value assignment shown:

| Performance | Points |
|---|---|
| Excellent (E) | 5 |
| Very good (VG) | 4 |
| Above average (G) | 3 |
| Average (Av) | 2 |
| Below average (F) | 1 |
| Poor (P) | 0 |
| Unknown (?) | 2 |

The last entry on the list applies when an appraiser has no valid opinion on an item. He simply marks it with a question mark and allows it two points.

By totaling the points given to each person appraised, a raw score is reached (maximum 100). However, since some appraisers are strict and some are lenient, this raw score cannot be used without risk. It's necessary to bring both lenient and strict appraisers in line with the company average. One way to accomplish this is to use deciles, that is, to rank all the employees rated by a given person on a scale of 1 to 10. For example, if each appraiser rated ten employees, the highest number of points he gave would be allowed a decile of 10 and the lowest a decile of 1. In that way, the person rated highest by the strictest appraiser would be in the same decile rank (10) as the person rated highest by the most lenient appraiser.

Of course, most groups will number fewer or more than ten employees. In such cases a conversion table such as Figure 12 can be used. For example, if that table were applied to a group of seven employees, the one receiving the highest raw score would be allowed a decile of 10, the next highest an 8, and so on. No one in this group would receive a 9, a 6, or a 4.

This conversion table can be used only when rating five or more persons. Its "probable error" is too great below this number. If a superior has only three subordinates, he can use the table by appraising at least two employees from other departments with whose work he is familiar.

*Figure 12. Table for converting ranks to deciles.*

Deciles

| Rank in Group According to Performance Rating | 5 | 6 | 7 | 8 | 9 | 10 | 11 | 12 | 13 | 14 | 15 | 16 | 17 | 18 | 19 | 20 |
|---|---|---|---|---|---|---|---|---|---|---|---|---|---|---|---|---|
| 1 | 10 | 10 | 10 | 10 | 10 | 10 | 10 | 10 | 10 | 10 | 10 | 10 | 10 | 10 | 10 | 10 |
| 2 | 8 | 8 | 8 | 8 | 8 | 9 | 9 | 9 | 9 | 9 | 10 | 10 | 10 | 10 | 10 | 10 |
| 3 | 6 | 6 | 7 | 7 | 7 | 8 | 8 | 8 | 8 | 8 | 9 | 9 | 9 | 9 | 9 | 9 |
| 4 | 3 | 4 | 5 | 6 | 6 | 7 | 7 | 7 | 8 | 8 | 8 | 8 | 9 | 9 | 9 | 9 |
| 5 | 1 | 2 | 3 | 4 | 5 | 6 | 6 | 6 | 7 | 7 | 7 | 7 | 8 | 8 | 8 | 8 |
| 6 | | 1 | 2 | 3 | 4 | 5 | 5 | 6 | 6 | 6 | 7 | 7 | 7 | 8 | 8 | 8 |
| 7 | | | 1 | 2 | 3 | 4 | 4 | 5 | 5 | 5 | 6 | 6 | 6 | 7 | 7 | 7 |
| 8 | | | | 1 | 2 | 3 | 3 | 4 | 4 | 5 | 5 | 6 | 6 | 7 | 7 | 7 |
| 9 | | | | | 1 | 2 | 2 | 3 | 3 | 4 | 4 | 5 | 5 | 6 | 6 | 6 |
| 10 | | | | | | 1 | 2 | 2 | 3 | 3 | 4 | 4 | 5 | 5 | 6 | 6 |
| 11 | | | | | | | 1 | 1 | 2 | 2 | 3 | 3 | 4 | 4 | 5 | 5 |
| 12 | | | | | | | | 1 | 1 | 2 | 2 | 3 | 3 | 4 | 4 | 5 |
| 13 | | | | | | | | | 1 | 1 | 2 | 2 | 3 | 3 | 4 | 4 |
| 14 | | | | | | | | | | 1 | 1 | 2 | 2 | 3 | 3 | 4 |
| 15 | | | | | | | | | | | 1 | 1 | 2 | 2 | 3 | 3 |
| 16 | | | | | | | | | | | | 1 | 1 | 2 | 2 | 3 |
| 17 | | | | | | | | | | | | | 1 | 1 | 2 | 2 |
| 18 | | | | | | | | | | | | | | 1 | 1 | 2 |
| 19 | | | | | | | | | | | | | | | 1 | 1 |
| 20 | | | | | | | | | | | | | | | | 1 |

Number of Members in Group

If several appraisers rate a large number of employees, it's possible to study the effectiveness of the table. When all rankings have been converted to deciles, there should be approximately 10 percent of employees who receive 10, 10 percent who receive 9, and so on.

Some managements do not believe in assigning numbers to performance. They prefer to describe performance in qualitative terms and to have appraisers recommend what further development of the person rated is needed. This recommendation can of course supplement any system.

## Appraisal and Motivation

There are hundreds of performance appraisal systems. Some are analytic and some are superficial. Different methods of administering performance appraisal systems are used. At White Motor Company the appraiser fills in the form, discusses it with his superiors, and then calls in the person appraised for a review. Citibank in New York, taking a different tack, lets the employee fill in the form himself. Then the self-appraisal is discussed between superior and subordinate. To guard against appraisers being too generous in their ratings, Western Electric allows no more than 20 percent "outstanding" ratings to be awarded by their supervisors. Virtually all systems guide management on wage and salary administration. They also help locate people ready for training or promotion and aim to prevent real talent from getting lost in the shuffle.

Wage and salary administration is a headache for almost all managers. Across-the-board increases have no motivation value since everyone benefits alike. Employees may be dissatisfied about inequities resulting from any system of job evaluation with performance appraisal. An administrator must satisfy himself that the system is fair.

Most managers agree that job performance should be the prime determinant of advancement, yet many managers have no method of measuring job performance. Others have no confidence in the accuracy of available data. Appraising is improved, and incentive added, if objective measures of performance are used. Once such standards are established, the performance appraisal becomes easier.

Labor shortages often cause managers to move employees through grades at more rapid rates than justified by the job evaluation and performance appraisal plan. Fast moves help keep employees from seeking other employment.

There are other motivational considerations which a manager should take into account. For one, the time lag between performance and reward often means that the employee doesn't see the relationship between the two. Thus, a profit sharing plan where an employee has to wait until the end of the year before he knows whether anything is due him has little incentive. And if the amount received from profit sharing is insignificant, he feels no motivation in the future. Further, if an employee is satisfied with his standard of living, he may not be motivated to improve production or quality to qualify for higher pay.

## Money as a Motivator

Some researchers classify earnings as weak motivators. Others say that the way money is dispensed determines its motivating power. It is true that not all people respond alike to money incentives. There's little doubt that inequitable handling of compensation causes *negative* motivation. Most successful compensation programs include:

Mathematical evaluation of jobs to put them into their proper grades.

Establishment of min and max rates for various grades.

Pay grades that overlap by about 50 percent. The midpoint of one is the minimum of the next higher grade.

Normal steps for progression from min to max—about 5 percent to 7 percent for each step.

A performance review period once each year, but more often with new, low-level employees.

Employees rated on job performance.

Performance rated on factors selected by an employee and his immediate supervisor from the job itself.

Standards of performance are set by joint agreement.

Bonus pay related to the basic job evaluation rate.

Repeated explanation to employees of how job evaluation with performance rating works.

## Fringe Benefits

These days most compensation plans include many fringe benefits. They may add as much as 25 percent to the employer's payroll costs.

Fringe benefits include life insurance, hospitalization insurance, sickness benefits, retirement pay, vacation pay, holiday pay, recreational and social activities, cafeterias, employer contributions to a savings plan, legal aid, personal counseling, loans, dental insurance, home nursing assistance.

While many people think these benefits are free, a wise aphorism asserts that "There is no such thing as a *free* lunch." Somebody, somewhere, pays. Their costs are reflected in the prices, so employees as consumers help pay these fringe costs.

The costs of fringe benefits are rising. This fact may influence decisions to make additional capital investments to reduce size of the work force. Other ways to reduce fringe benefit costs are:

- ☐ Study insurance policies for ways to avoid premium increases.
- ☐ Avoid allowing a fixed number of sick-leave days per year.
- ☐ Close the entire plant for a vacation in a slack season.
- ☐ When adding a holiday, designate a slack time.
- ☐ Relate vacation to length of service.
- ☐ In collective bargaining, insist on productivity gains as a prerequisite for added benefits.
- ☐ Avoid the device of increasing fringe benefits in order to pirate employees from other employers.
- ☐ Keep employees informed about costs, benefits, and abuses.

Fringe benefits provide little incentive to higher production or better quality. Employees consider benefits a right, not extra compensation. They are now so much a part of our social fabric that they are considered an obligation of the business world to society.

## REVIEW

Name two systems of job evaluation.

Aside from job difficulty, what other influences affect wage rates?

Name at least five factors found in a point system of job evaluation.

Describe a key scale used in factor comparison.

Name six items used in a performance appraisal.

Name six fringe benefits.

# 7

# MOTIVATION: PROVING GROUND FOR MANAGERS

Getting things done through people has always been a manager's most important job. Whether he uses coercion or persuasion, command or participation, motivation has been a manager's most challenging assignment and the ultimate test of his ability. Attitudes toward work do not run in cycles as predictable as the changing tides. Yet it is changing attitudes toward work that make altering the motivating game plan essential.

## How Attitudes Have Changed

The industrial revolution changed society in many countries from agrarian to industrial. As nations prospered, work became acceptable for all social levels. In fact, those who would not work were regarded as social parasites. The dignity of human labor became the cornerstone of social philosophy.

Currently, a number of influences seem to be downgrading the importance of productive work:

Automation, which produces goods superior to those made by man.
Rising affluence of workers.
Subdivision of labor causing dull, repetitive, even degrading work.

Labor shortages.
Increasing mobility of labor.
Shorter work weeks, resulting in more time for outside interests.
Higher education.
Increasing proportion of younger workers.
Lessening social stigma attached to being unemployed.
Welfare programs which have dulled financial incentives to find work.
A sharp increase in the ratio of persons employed in service industries as compared to manufacturing.
Decline in loyalty to any one employer.

No one can be sure of the end result of the interplay of these forces. Here are some predictions:

Work will be a less important aspect of our future lives.
New activities will be developed for work-free hours.
New goals for ego satisfaction will be needed, so providing new types of motivation.
Man will pay greater attention to the social sciences to avoid destroying himself by poor uses of the physical sciences.
Managers will assume the lead in finding solutions to many social problems.

## Blue Collar Blues

"Blue collar blues" is a term used to describe new attitudes of many hourly-paid employees. It has been called a revolt, a silent strike, or a reaction against assembly line, dehumanizing work. Surveys by research groups reveal growing disenchantment with jobs among plant employees, clerks, and retail workers. Some studies suggest a similar disaffection among foremen, technicians, and middle management.

One sign of discontent is rapid labor turnover. Some of it results from disappointment when expectations are not realized. Additional psychological pressure may result from indifference of fellow employees or lack of attention from supervisors during the crucial first weeks of employment.

Some managers deny that the assembly line is to blame for new worker attitudes. They assert that workers are no more bored than in the past. They criticize writers for sensationalism augmented by the use of catch words like "blue collar blues." They believe that proposed solutions will raise costs of production, lessen ability to compete in international markets, and contribute to inflation. Even some union leaders say that descriptions of work conditions as dehumanizing are grossly exaggerated. However, whatever the causes, there can be no doubt that workers' interest in their jobs has fallen.

Job dissatisfaction takes its toll in health of employees and managers. Stomach ulcers, spastic colons, coronary heart disease, and strokes are much higher for the work-weary than for those who are job-happy. Job stress causes higher adrenalin release, more rapid heartbeat, higher blood pressure, increased digestive secretions, and a higher cholesterol level. Job stress may be caused by the nature of the task: boring, too easy, too difficult, too many decisions, too heavy, disagreeable. Other causes of stress may be the job environment; frictions with fellow workers; too much, too little, or annoying supervision; and inequitable compensation.

No manager can hope to make all employees happy in their jobs all the time. He can, however, note continuing dissatisfaction and consider whether counseling, more training, encouragement, job enrichment, better supervision, wage increases, transfer, or help from fellow employees would decrease emotional pressures.

Aggressive employees are more likely to suffer ulcers, heart disease, or high blood pressure than those who are easygoing. Aggression is an attitude which, like many attitudes, can be changed or redirected by good managers.

## Overcoming Employee Apathy

Man is a working animal, happy when he is doing something useful. The industrial malaise known as *employee apathy* indicates that many employees do not feel they are doing something useful.

Employee job expectations include security, good working conditions, congenial associates, reasonable hours, fair wages, higher wages, meaningful work, recognition, opportunities to advance, freedom of action, and capable leadership.

These needs vary with individuals and change with different periods in their lives. Whether a given job will satisfy important needs depends on the education, intelligence, skill, health, and ambition of the job holder.

A helpful approach to overcome employee apathy can be preparation of a "man-job analysis" for each worker, beginning with those jobs where the greatest turnover occurs. First-line supervisors can be taught to make such analyses by observation and friendly interviews with each employee. Man-job analysis helps to adjust employees' abilities and interests to job requirements, or, occasionally, to adjust jobs to fit employees.

Frequently, the first-line supervisors who prepare man-job analyses benefit as much as their subordinates. Job analysis and interviews often result in eliminating work irritants. Working conditions or methods are improved as tasks are realigned. Supervisors better come to understand workers' emotional needs, and employees learn to know themselves. Closer relationships develop between employees and supervisors, and this closeness often results in reduced absenteeism and turnover.

Such a program is not a panacea for *all* employee apathy. But it will overcome a substantial portion of it.

## Employee Needs and Job Satisfaction

The most widely accepted classification of human needs is the five-level hierarchy proposed by Abraham Maslow, which is illustrated in Figure 13. The lower-level needs, the physiological and safety needs, are those that are essential to all human beings, whether civilized or primitive. However, in developed societies those basic needs are less pressing and the higher-level needs become more important. Here are some subdivisions of the five levels of need:

Level 5, *self-actualization:* accomplishment, self-fulfillment, opportunity for continued growth and self-expression.

Level 4, *self-esteem:* status, prestige, recognition, sense of worthwhileness.

Level 3, *social:* acceptance by the group, friendships, love, helping others.

Level 2, *safety:* protection against physical hazards, threats, or job insecurity.

Level 1, *physiological:* water, food, shelter, sex, muscular activity, bodily comfort.

*Figure 13. Maslow's hierarchy of needs.*

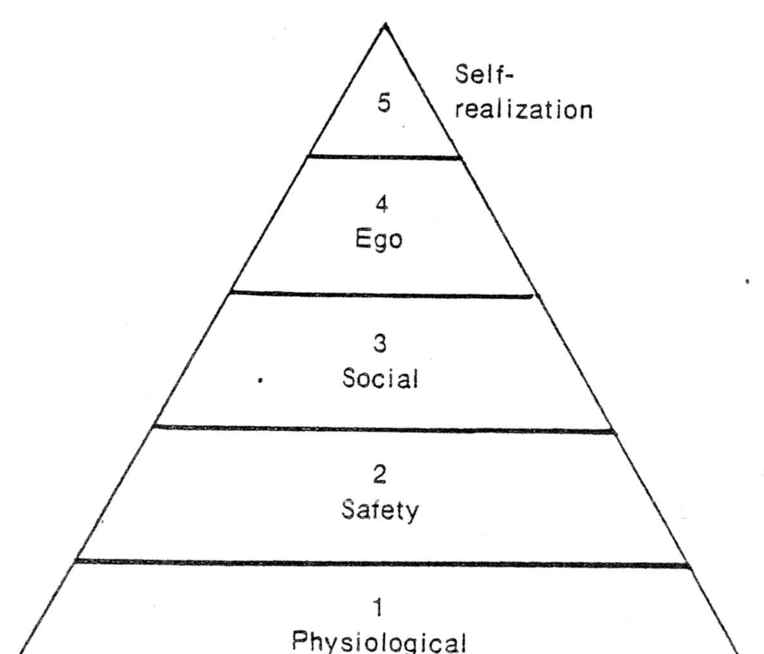


Since industrial organizations have largely met the two lowest levels, better educated employees look to the three highest levels for job satisfactions. Man becomes, therefore, a perpetually wanting animal, as most employers have discovered. Many employers make the mistake of trying to motivate employees through already satisfied lower-level needs.

Employees, groping for satisfaction of their higher needs, express their wants in terms of more money. They see more dollars as balms for wounded egos or frustrated needs, or as a way to purchase higher-level satisfactions outside the company. The next two chapters show how some of these satisfiers can be made available in the work situation.

## THEORY X VERSUS THEORY Y

When Douglas McGregor wrote his book *The Human Side of Enterprise,* he threw a bombshell into the field of management because of his exposition of Theory X and Theory Y.

Theory X assumes that workers are passive, unimaginative, uninterested in their jobs, greedy for money and security, lacking in ambition or a sense of responsibility, and in need of strict authoritarian leadership.

Theory Y proposes that people want to work, that under the right conditions they can assume responsibility, think creatively, be goal-directed, and exercise self-direction in job performance.

Some managers cite these conditions which support Theory X: absenteeism, lateness, labor turnover, apathy, indifference to quality, inflationary wage demands, insolence, and insubordination. These employee deficiencies, say the managers, make necessary detailed standard practice instructions, tight rules, penalties, rigid inspection, and close supervision.

Behavioral scientists contend that authoritarian management practices are largely responsible for these conditions, helped by more education, better communications, advertising, radio, television, affluence, and higher cultural standards.

Currently many managers blend the two theories, occasionally experimenting with Theory Y for individuals or small groups. The thrust of the future will undeniably be toward an extension of the Y philosophy.

## HERZBERG'S FINDINGS

After extensive research, Frederick Herzberg distinguished between "hygiene factors" and "motivators." In the former category he placed wages, fringe benefits, working conditions, company policies, and the kind of supervision provided. They are the climate under which the job is performed and can prevent dissatisfaction. They are expected to be good as a matter of employee right. Hygiene factors do not stimulate to higher effort although their absence can contribute to negative motivation.

Motivators are challenging tasks, new experiences, opportunity for growth and advancement, status, and expectation of achievement and recognition. Their absence leads to dissatisfaction.

Managers tend to resist the theories and findings of behavioral scientists. They may feel threatened by critical inquiries, new concepts, or challenges to stereotyped, comfortable modes of thought. They use derogatory labels like "impractical" or "ivory tower" to cover up their unwillingness to keep an open mind toward new ideas.

## Motivating Employees

In its broadest sense, motivation can be defined as anything which changes behavior. The instigating cause could be the prick of a pin, freezing cold temperature, the loss of a loved one, or the demagoguery of a Hitler.

Managers motivate by taking actions to cause employees, supervisors, customers, and others to behave in a manner favorable to the business. How to motivate employees is receiving increasing attention from managers. Motivation does not mean manipulation, which employees soon recognize and resent.

Motivation can be either financial or nonfinancial. Some authorities prefer the words "tangible" or "intangible."

Most managers consider money and fringe benefits as motivators. Most sociologists agree but insist that how such rewards are dispensed is extremely important. They also say that money has its greatest motivating power with employees whose desire for achievement is low.

Employees with high achievement needs, say the scientists, like to face work-challenge. Money rewards offer proof of winning as well as providing the means to buy necessities and outside satisfactions. High achievers spend time prudently and try to meet not only the standards set by society and their superiors, but the high standards they set for themselves. They have a habit of meeting their obligations promptly. Typically they come from the economic middle class rather than from either the upper or lower classes. Obviously it's important for managers to be able to spot high achievers among subordinates.

At IBM's General Products Division laboratory in Boulder, Colorado, employees are recognized for their creativity and accomplishments through a unique Creativity/Accomplishment (C/A) program. To stimulate employee awareness, all publicity having to do with the program carries a "trademark" consisting of two abstract, yet easily recognizable symbols: a stylized octagonal star representing the spark of creativity, and an exploded square representing accomplishment. The two symbols can be displayed side by side, or with the star transposed into the open spaces of the exploded square to denote the completion of a creative effort. The symbols appear in a series of posters and in three-dimensional displays throughout the laboratory.

The following accomplishments qualify an employee for recognition:

Patent activity
Publishing a technical article or report
Presenting a technical conference paper
Receiving an award in another company program

Candid photographs of recipients are displayed at prominent locations in the laboratory accompanied by a brief description of the accomplishment. A short article is also printed in the employee newspaper.

The highlight of the program is the annual C/A dinner held in the grand ballroom of a local hotel. Here the recipients are dined, entertained, and recognized for their contributions.

The company believes that the program has been a decided success in stimulating employees to reach for high creativity and accomplishment.

**Individual and Group Motivators**

Group motivators appeal to team spirit, to the tendency to form a united front to face opposition, to the need for acceptance by other members, or to the joy of team accomplishment. Individual motivation requires understanding of the person's emotional needs. Which have been satisfied? Which are now pressing for satisfaction?

The main devices for motivating subordinates are words, situations, standards, symbols, goals, and actions.

Some words are power-packed, as advertisers and salesmen have long since learned. Curses are negatively, praise is positively, power-packed. Criticism in the presence of fellow workers is negative, but helpful coaching in private can be positive. Standards can challenge, especially if employees have helped establish them. Status symbols are often strong motivators—private office, important title, or even a key to the executive washroom!

To motivate, goals must be worthwhile, specific, and attainable. Employees must believe that management knows how to achieve them. Goals which present great challenges yield strong satisfactions when they are achieved.

Finally, the actions of a leader can provide positive or negative motivation to his followers. He must not say one thing and do another, nor make promises he does not fulfill. By good planning, prompt decisions, support of subordinates, and continued encouragement, a manager can provide strong motivation through personal example.

Motivation can be in the nature of rewards or punishments. Rewards can be tangible (money, medal, plaque, ribbon, etc.) or intangible (expectation of future benefit, praise, involvement, acceptance, or satisfaction of a felt need). Punishments can be the taking away of rewards, denial of satisfactions, assignment of unpleasant tasks, and the like. Most individuals are more strongly motivated by rewards than punishments. A motivator (reward or punishment) is most effective when it comes soon after the action that inspired it. The longer the time lapse between action and motivator, the less effective the motivator.

Here are some motivating practices that managers have found helpful:

☐ Recognition

1. Praise the *work* and not the worker. The employee feels he is being praised and so is motivated to repeat the good work. At the same time, his fellow employees may be motivated to follow his example. Praise of the *worker,* on the other hand, may cause jealousy or suspicion of favoritism.
2. Praise the work in the presence of others, not in private.
3. Call each employee *by name* the first time you see him each day.
4. Show respect for all subordinates, even those who are less informed or less skilled.

☐ Participation

5. Ask advice and help from subordinates, especially in setting goals.

6. Listen carefully to suggestions or complaints, and show understanding. Get all needed facts. Explain your decisions.
7. Be a coordinator rather than a slave driver.

☐ Competition

8. Pit group against group rather than employee against employee.
9. Compare an employee's performance against some standard, not against some other worker. Comparison with another worker can lead to friction.
10. Announce in advance rewards for winning a competition.

☐ Discipline

11. Hold each employee accountable for specific results.
12. Criticize methods or results, not intentions. In analyzing failure, ask questions. Do not accuse, belittle, or compare. The interview should be private.
13. To criticize some specific practice, use the "sandwich technique": Praise some minor point, comment on the point being criticized, praise some related point.
14. In disputes seek what is right, not who.
15. Disciplinary actions should be fair, firm, and consistent.

**Motivating Supervisors**

Supervisors have the same basic needs as other employees, plus some special needs relating to their special responsibilities. If these needs are met by wise superiors, motivation results.

Aside from monetary rewards, supervisors want to see their responsibilities spelled out in a job description. They need to know the extent of their authority to hire, fire, spend money, make work decisions, change methods, confer with other departments, and the like. They are entitled to report to one superior only.

On the Maslow scale of needs, most middle managers have passed the first three levels (physiological, safety, and social) and are at the fourth level—self-esteem, personal worth, independence. Some are reaching for the fifth level—self-fulfillment, continued development, creativeness.

Any superior who can find ways to satisfy these higher-level desires will surely enjoy high loyalty and performance in return.

## REVIEW

Name five influences on changing attitudes toward productive work.

Name some diseases caused or aggravated by job stress.

What can a manager do to overcome employee apathy?

Distinguish between McGregor's theory X and theory Y.

Name some of Herzberg's hygiene factors.

Why should a manager praise the work and not the worker?

# 8

# COMMUNICATION: MANAGEMENT'S PIVOTAL ART

One of the problems of modern management is that business has a poor public image—and the situation has been getting worse. Studies of Opinion Research Corporation show that over half the population has a low opinion of business. Three out of four people believe in tougher government policies toward business. Pollution, rising prices, bad working conditions, failure to employ minority applicants, defective products, excessive profits, and lack of social responsibility are among faults laid at the door of business.

Opinion polls show that the average American believes that U.S. companies net 28 percent profit on sales. The fact is that the average is less than 4 percent. Even giant corporations average less than 6 percent net profit on sales.

## INDUSTRY SHOULD TELL ITS STORY

For many years companies have been urged to tell their story to the American public. Some have tried to do so with little success. So unless managers start telling the story more effectively, the free enterprise system may weaken or even collapse.

Consider some facts. Business pays a major part of all taxes. The dividends distributed to stockholders result in income taxes paid by them. The most profitable companies are able to pay the highest wages and offer the best fringe benefits. Successful companies keep the United States competitive in world markets. Business gives financial support to many charitable organizations. Many executives give time and money to community projects.

Telling industry's story to the general public takes deeds as well as words. Managers will need closer contact with schools to start economic understanding in lower grades. Workers with only a few years of high school have not learned how the free enterprise system operates. No wonder they feel out of the mainstream! Since our economic system is strange to them, they fear it. This gap in understanding is not confined to attitudes toward business. It exists also in attitudes toward government, education, medicine, and religion. However, business and industry suffer the most.

The critics of the American free enterprise system are very vocal. It is time that managers become equally vocal. This is an important management challenge. Management has contacts with at least four publics: customers, stockholders, vendors, and employees. These four can be very influential in projecting a company's image.

## Communication with Customers

Companies make strong efforts to communicate well with customers. Some of this communication occurs through advertising and selling. To the extent that these are backed up by good products and services, they represent good communication. On the other hand, some TV commercials and print ads lessen company credibility or even annoy.

With customers there's no substitute for face-to-face communication. Retail sales people can attract or drive away customers by their words and attitudes. Much the same can be said for wholesale salesmen when contacting dealers or training dealer salesmen. So companies should emphasize sales training. This training should include information about the arts of communication as well as product knowledge.

## Communication with Stockholders

Many managements act as though stockholders were a necessary nuisance. In truth, the stockholders own the company. Some high-level managers ignore or deceive directors. But they are the elected representatives of the owners of the business. Such actions are grave communication mistakes.

To improve communications, an increasing number of companies are sending out quarterly stockholder reports. These reports are becoming more frank, giving negative as well as positive information. Stockholders are becoming more sophisticated in reading financial statements. They are also part of the general public, and for this reason too managements must maintain honest communications with them.

## Communication with Vendors

Some companies treat vendors as second-class citizens. They act as though they were doing the vendor a favor by purchasing his goods. But companies could not operate without the products and services supplied by their vendors.

Bad communication with vendors can have consequences on the company's credit rating. To improve relations, some companies offer free assistance to vendors on legal matters, accounting, advertising, market research and other aspects of successful management. These aids are more than communication—they're goodwill builders.

## Communication with Employees

Employee communications informs and persuades employees. When well done, it motivates. There should be five-way employee communications, as illustrated in Figure 14. The first is from the top down. Too often this is merely one-way communication—when the man at the top believes that his message will result in the desired action. However modern managers use feedback to make sure that their directions are understood and carried out. This is two-way.

The third way carries suggestions or complaints upward from the employee. Because the employee often never learns what has happened to his ideas, the fourth way of communication should be

*Figure 14. Five-way employee communications.*

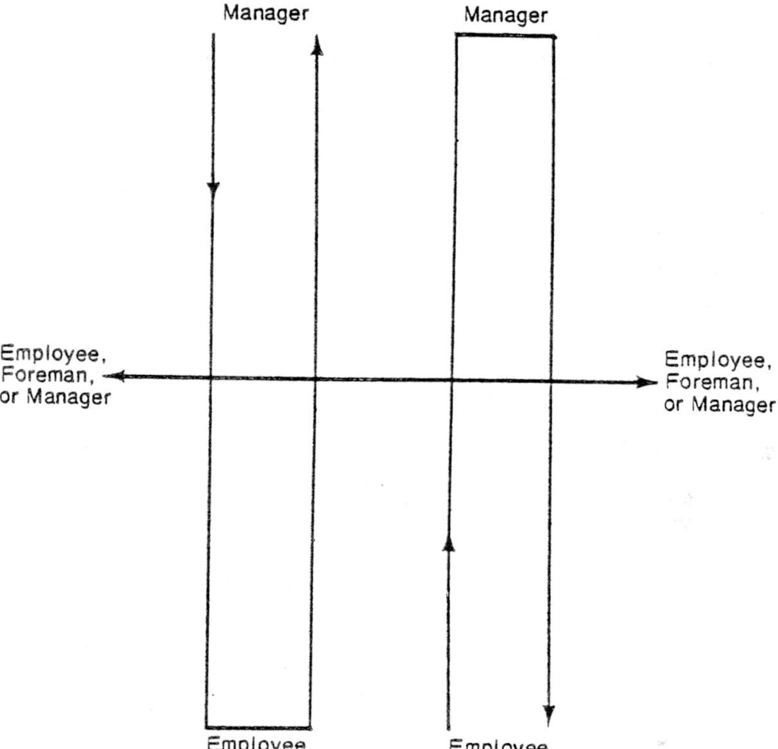


another feedback process: The manager should let the employee know that his communication has been understood and answer his complaint or suggestion. The fifth path of communication is lateral—from employee to employee, from foreman to foreman, or from department head to department head.

Often something is lost in upward transmission. This happens when the message is either distorted by the opinions of someone in the communication chain or blocked by a poor listener. Many managers don't know how to listen. One poor listener not only can stop the message from moving upward in the communication chain, he can also keep employees from talking freely in the future.

If an employee brings a problem to a poor listener, the employee's self-image is challenged. The problem then becomes even more acute. However, if he talks to an understanding superior, he maintains his self-image and leaves feeling better. Sometimes just talking about a complaint is enough to end it.

A good listener pays full attention. He will have to decide if an idea is worthwhile or a complaint is justified. To show he understands, the manager will repeat what the speaker says. If the employee agrees, then there has indeed been two-way communication. At this point, good managers will avoid appearing to give a snap judgment. If a manager needs time to reach a decision, he will set a time for his answer. In this event he must make sure that he does answer at the promised time.

Dr. Rudolph Flesch, a specialist in words and communication, suggests that to be effective, communicators should:

Use familiar words in place of the unfamiliar.
Use concrete words in place of the abstract.
Use short words in place of long.
Use single words in place of several.

Status affects communication especially in rigidly formed hierarchical organizations characteristic of many corporations. Prestige, power, position, title, and money can confer status on an individual regardless of his abilities. So people who have status should unbend when communicating with subordinates.

A famous advertising man, Arthur Kudner, wrote these words to his son: "All big things have little names such as life and death, peace and war, or dawn, day, night, hope, love, home. Learn to use little words in a big way. It is hard to do, but they say what you mean. When you don't know what you mean—use big words; they often fool little people."

A speaker on radio is an example of one-way communication. No matter how carefully he plans his message, he can never be sure whether his listeners understood or took action because of what he said. Put this same speaker before a class and the students may raise questions. This is two-way communication. By means of two-way communication speakers learn that they have to repeat or rephrase some ideas. They also learn that audiences do not listen continuously.

One-way communication is easy on speakers or writers. Unfortunately, they may not actually be communicating but rather merely expressing themselves. Two-way communication sometimes can be exasperating, but in the end it provides real give and take.

The executive who proudly announces, "My door is always open" has really not established two-way communication. The initiative should be his for the most part and not his employees'. So he should circulate freely among them, ask questions, give ideas, elicit comments, and make it clear that he is open to suggestions, complaints, and requests for information. Until he establishes freedom of communication, no manager can be certain that the channels are open.

Moreover, subordinates tend to keep negative information from management, preferring to try to deal with any difficulties themselves. They fear criticism or loss of a chance for promotion if they admit oversight, carelessness, or inaction. To test whether communication channels are open, the superior seeks feedback. If it is negative, he accepts it gracefully without condemnation or emotional display. Managers find useful a rule to look for what is right rather than who. Building confidence between subordinates and superiors makes it much easier to get at the truth.

The Hickory Manufacturing Company of Hickory, North Carolina, makers of quality furniture, has had outstanding success with a down-to-earth plan of employee communication. Each Wednesday the vice president of manufacturing meets with ten employees for one hour to answer any questions they may have and to inform them about plans and progress of the company. The meeting is followed by a one-hour guided tour, covering all departments of the plant.

The vice president states that the questions raised cover profit sharing, insurance, vacation plan, lunchroom, and other fringe benefits, as well as the job evaluation plan and various management practices.

Hickory's management says that the program "has accomplished to the fullest the desired goals" of free communication between employees and management.

The Riverside, California, plant of Alcan Aluminum Corporation was forced to cut its forces from 1200 to 600 employees because of loss of defense business. To offset lowered morale, management established "operation speakeasy." Under this plan, employees signed up in groups of three to have lunch in the cafeteria with a senior manager. The union cooperated in the program.

Employees asked questions or volunteered comments. Eventually 80 percent of employees participated. The main topics discussed were:

| | |
|---|---|
| Productivity and ways to improve it | 32% |
| Causes of low morale | 26% |
| Poor communications | 23% |
| Work environment | 18% |

The company issued 30 bulletins on various issues. It gave actions to be taken and explained why certain actions were not desirable or practical. Morale and productivity rose, presumably as a result. However, the plan did not become a continuing personnel program. It had been designed strictly to offset the chaotic conditions resulting from a drastic reduction in work force. And such a program, as the director of industrial relations said "should be used to solve a specific problem, be limited to a . . . stated period of time, and not be repeated for several years. . . ."

By developing understanding, senders and receivers of communication reach the point where, when one-way communication proves necessary, the receivers will obey instructions without question.

## Communication with Subgroups

Communication in a company often calls for relationships between a superior and several subgroups. Each subgroup has its own goals and ways of achieving them, its own interpretation of communications from above, and its own means of internal communication. Groupings may be by profession, occupation, sex, union membership, or even by age. The degree of friendliness among members of a given group may influence the reception given a communication from the top. If there is internal dissension, superiors may have to treat members of the group as individuals. Where there is an obvious group leader, superiors will inform and persuade him.

In addition to the formal lines of communication within an organization, there is always an informal or grapevine system. The grapevine includes people who share personal contacts and friendships. Much of the communication flow within this system is beyond the reach of a manager, but he should be aware that it exists. The grapevine can help information flows though it's more susceptible to misinformation.

In any work group the best workers and the poorest workers get more supervisory communication than the others, but for different reasons. Most managers communicate less than they think they do and are surprised when things go wrong. Attitude surveys in many companies have revealed that employees want more communication than they now get. Surveys also show that improved transmitting and receiving of information raises morale and performance.

Good communications are not a remedy for all organization ailments. But they are important tools and ones which are often neglected in many companies.

When communication breaks down, a manager should try to build greater trust between himself and his employees. He should analyze rather than condemn when given negative information. Finally, he should explain organization purpose and policy, and involve employees in departmental goal setting so they will see how they fit in. He can show them that what is good for the organization is also good for them.

## Written Communication

Much business communication originates in written form. Writing it down may force the manager to think through exactly what he wants to communicate. However, the manager should first test what he has written on a few people to find out if it is clear or open to misinterpretation. Feedback tells a writer if the thoughts he tried to put down on paper are the same thoughts that came into the minds of the readers. One authority, Dr. S. I. Hayakawa, said, "The meanings of words are not in the words; they are in us."

Written communication from management should be followed up by as much personal contact between top managers and those affected as time permits. In these contacts good speech habits and vocabulary are important. So are logical and rational presentations of ideas. A good written communication can be badly distorted by a poor oral follow-up.

## The Optimum Pace

A little-understood principle is that of the *optimum pace*. Time study people have long since discovered that if an employee is forced to work faster than his optimum pace he can do so for a short period. After that he becomes frustrated or fatigued and makes errors or simply refuses to keep up the higher pace. If he works slower than his optimum pace, he may daydream, socialize, become careless, or show signs of false fatigue.

The principle of optimum pace is applicable to physical work in the plant, mental work in the office, creative work in the laboratory, or sales calls in the field.

Closely related to optimum pace is the rate at which information is communicated and the complexity of decisions that have to be made. Usually new employees have ideas and management's decisions thrust upon them too rapidly—with negative consequences. A sensible manager tries to keep his demands in line with his employees' optimum work pace, their ability to absorb the knowledge communicated to them, and their ability to take the actions asked of them.

## Empire Building versus Communication

Empire building can set up rivalries which interfere with the free flow of a company's lateral communications. In one large company the sales manager and production manager had chosen not to speak to each other for a year. They would volunteer information to the executive vice president in a meeting, but that was all. As a consequence, employees in the two departments adopted the same attitude and lateral communication between two important functions of this company disappeared. An unseen barrier to communication had been erected, not only at the top management level but at lower levels as well.

In a situation like this, lower-level managers are badly handicapped. They cannot go to their superiors and ask for permission to contact the other department. On the other hand, if they go directly to the other department, they are likely to get the cold shoulder. Such a situation should be corrected as quickly as possible by bringing it to the attention of the highest authority.

## Employee Attitude Surveys

Employee attitude surveys provide feedback communication in industrial relations. In a typical survey each employee checks off multiple-choice answers. An unsigned questionnnaire asks 30 or more questions on attitudes toward job, boss, and company. Results are tabulated and percentages computed for each question by department, shift, sex, age, and length of service.

Such surveys are a healthy means of communication between employees and top management, providing such advantages as:

1. Draining complaints from workers with grievances.
2. Revealing practices, policies, supervisors, tasks, or working conditions which are causing irritation.
3. Pinpointing such irritations by department or shift.
4. Identifying which groups—but not which employees—are alienated: men or women, young or old, new or long-service employees.
5. Uncovering voluntary suggestions.

Typical findings of an attitude survey might be:

Employees in the upholstery department dislike the lighting and the way the foreman handles complaints and consider the piece rates unfair.

The second shift has high morale.

New employees have better morale than those with five to nine years' service.

Women employees have higher morale than men.

Employees would like the parking lot paved.

Careful analysis of the survey's findings can be used to develop a program aimed at eliminating weaknesses uncovered. Such a program might include supervisory training, improvements in working conditions, policy changes, correction of misunderstandings, greater employee participation, or other specific actions.

The more employees and supervisors who can be involved in the improvement program, the greater will be its acceptance. Obviously, if management fails to take action—or even only seems not to act—the morale of employees may drop even lower than it was before the survey.

The Saga Administrative Corporation of Menlo Park, California, has used findings from an unsigned attitude survey of managers as the basis for instituting an organization development (OD) program. Discussion teams at all levels considered the survey findings, presented complaints, offered suggestions for betterment. The effort turned into a continuing and ramified process of free communication between employees and their supervisors, and between supervisors and top managers. OD is now an accepted part of the company's management fabric.

## Flow of Information

Supplying information to managers is a form of communication. The glossary in Chapter 1 defines a management information system as "an organized procedure to supply executives with information pertinent to their assignments." To achieve this end, a number of steps should be taken:

1. A study should be made to determine what information is needed by each manager. Some managers merely accept data supplied them without considering what additional information, if any, could be helpful.
2. Methods should be set up to gather information, to organize it, and to get it to users in time to be of value. Charts may help.
3. Where possible, standards of performance should be applied by users. Examples of such standards are standard times, standard costs, budgets, historical averages, and minimum acceptable figures.
4. Feedback to a superior is essential. The subordinate explains low figures or tells what action he is taking to correct bad situations revealed by the data.

Information flow has been likened to the human nervous system. There is input, central data processing, and output in both systems. However, the human body has associative interconnections; for example, the pores of the skin open automatically in response to a rise in air temperature. This automatic feature is missing in business information flow. For instance, production may not be fully aware of what sales is doing, and vice versa. Management should evaluate its information flow on a regular basis—perhaps when compiling the annual budget.

## REVIEW

What percent net profit on sales does the average U.S. business earn?

Why is good communication with vendors important?

Name five channels of communication in an organization.

In listening to an employee complaint, what should a superior do?

Why is written communication desirable?

What is meant by the term "optimum pace?"

How is an employee attitude survey conducted?

# 9

# MODERN EMPLOYEE RELATIONS PRACTICES

A furniture manufacturer once said, "My business is 10 percent wood, 10 percent machines, and 80 percent people." Waking up to the importance of people in business is causing vast changes in management practice, especially in motivation, communication, and other employee relationships. Many companies have tested working hour changes, tried to make jobs more meaningful, and applied a results approach to personnel practices.

## Combating Lateness

Employee lateness has been one factor in bringing about changes in working hours. Most companies are plagued with chronic offenders. When management can't break up late arrivals, other employees catch the habit. At worst, one late worker may hold up an entire assembly line. At best, he handicaps the other people on the line.

Office employees in particular think they aren't bound by specific reporting times. Frequently they claim voluntary overtime as an offset to lateness.

Companies haven't had much success with penalty systems. Some concerns offer small bonuses for nearly perfect on-time records. Sometimes the offender is so important to departmental production that his supervisor feels he can't risk applying disciplinary measures. Yet if he disciplines some less valuable employee, he's accused of favoritism.

Since most of the lateness problem occurs with repeaters, the best results have come from friendly counseling—set the alarm clock 15 minutes earlier, take an earlier bus, join a different car pool. If relationships between the employee and his supervisor are close, a personal appeal to loyalty may be enough.

## PART-TIME EMPLOYMENT

As a step toward improved handling of employee relations problems such as lateness, some companies are using part-time employees for certain jobs that can be handled in shorter hours. Additional employees can be recruited to work such hours. For example, a housewife with family obligations may be able to work from 10 A.M. to 3 P.M. A retired person might be able to work short hours. College students, schoolteachers, postmen, or shift firemen may be able to put in ten or 20 moonlighting hours per week. These people become permanent part-time employees. Using part-time employees raises a number of questions:

1. Are part-time employees eligible for fringe benefits—paid vacations, insurance, retirement, profit sharing, and others?
2. Should the company assist part-timers in transportation, child care, loans?
3. Should part-time employees be allowed to vote in a union election?
4. Should they receive time and a half for working Saturdays, Sundays, or holidays?
5. Should some present full-time employees be permitted to change to a part-time status?
6. Does management clearly understand its obligations to such part-time employees for accident compensation, safety and health rules, discrimination, wage and hour laws, and other possible liabilities?
7. Which jobs do not lend themselves to part-time work?
8. What is the morale effect of part-timers on full-time employees?

## THE FOUR-DAY WORK WEEK

The first settlers in America worked from sunup to sundown. With each succeeding generation, the length of the work day and the work week decreased. In the 1930's the 40-hour week became the rule. Most companies discontinued regular Saturday work. The number of paid holidays in the year increased. Many were switched to Monday to make long weekends. In many companies, especially in offices, the 40-hour week was reduced to 35 hours.

Another step in improving employee relationships by changing working hours has been the four-day work week. Four ten-hour days have been tried. Some companies have tried three 12-hour days. Others tried four nine-hour days plus one four-hour day.

Employee reactions have been mixed. Some employees like the extra day off and the reduction in travel time and expense. Others feel that a 9½- or 10-hour work day is too tiring. It's still too early to tell whether the shorter work week will become permanent.

Change of any kind encounters resistance from some individuals. Hence it is no surprise that not all conversions to a four-day work week have proven successful. One furniture company, after a six months' trial, reverted to the five-day week because of belligerent opposition from employees. The Bowery Savings Bank of New York suspended the plan in two of five departments where it was being tried. The company concluded that the advantages outweighed the disadvantages and expects the program to be extended and to grow in employee acceptance.

Employers tend to like the four-day, ten-hour plan. It has helped recruit employees in labor-scale areas. Morale has improved. By scheduling two shifts of four-day workers, some employers get fuller utilization of equipment or provide longer hours for customer service. Absenteeism, turnover, and lateness have usually decreased. A study of four-day work week companies by the American Management Associations revealed improved production and reduced costs.

Smaller companies seem able to adjust to the four-day work week more easily than the giants.

Organized labor, which fought for the eight-hour day, finds the ten-hour day unacceptable. Some labor leaders, however, believe that the four-day week is inevitable because it meets with the approval of so many union members. Consequently those leaders are seeking a nine-hour-day, four-day work week.

## FLEXTIME

Some years ago European companies, faced with labor shortages, experimented with flexible working hours. Typically, each employee must work the "core hours" but may report any time between 8 A.M. and 10 A.M., and leave any time between 3 P.M. and 5 P.M. Between 10 A.M. and 3 P.M. all employees must be present. These are core hours. In a week, employees must put in the required number of hours.

On a production line, flextime can be used when all employees on the line agree on a common starting and stopping time. Alternatively, there may be experienced employees who are sufficiently versatile so that they can fill in during the flexible part of the working hours.

The Hewlett-Packard Company, headquartered in Palo Alto, California, makes the flexible work schedule available at its many plants. An employee can begin work between 6:30 and 8:30 A.M. and leave between 3:15 and 5:15 P.M. after completing an eight-hour work day. Certain modifications have proven necessary because of the nature of some jobs. The company considers the program very successful.

Different industries and different companies have problems which must be ironed out before part-time employees, the four-day work week or flextime can be used profitably. One thing seems certain: A shorter work week resulting in more leisure time is inevitable.

## MAKING JOBS MORE MEANINGFUL

Most experts in management-employee relationships agree that work must be made more *meaningful* to workers. Mechanization, the assembly line, and automation have eliminated the joy of craftsmanship from millions of jobs. At the same time these technological innovations have added to employee earnings. The combination promotes turnover, absenteeism, and employee apathy.

To restore "meaningfulness" to work, companies are trying techniques such as job enrichment and departmental teams. These techniques require retraining employees to handle the enlarged tasks and to qualify some for higher duties.

Involvement is the key to meaningful work. It shows itself in dedication, cooperation, and changed attitudes toward work and employers, especially when immediate supervisors are capable and cooperative.

## Job Enrichment

In situations where the work allows and job holders are equal to it, many companies are using job enlargement and job enrichment.

Job enlargement brings together a greater variety of tasks of about the same degree of difficulty. If ten employees on an assembly line are performing ten distinct operations, job enlargement calls for each worker to do all ten tasks on a given assembly.

Job enrichment means adding to a job responsibilities and controls formerly reserved to a higher level. These additions are called "vertical loading." They enrich a job by increasing the job holder's autonomy. Ways to increase autonomy include:

Reduction of unnecessary, duplicated, or ineffective external controls.
Addition of management functions.
Addition of more challenging technical tasks.
Granting of new authority.
More responsibility for time management.
More authority to "trouble shoot" and make decisions in times of crisis.
Greater control over budgeting and other financial aspects of nonfinancial jobs.

A job enrichment program involving maintenance employees at the Ravenswood, West Virginia, smelter of Kaiser Aluminum & Chemical Corp. reduced total maintenance costs 5.5 percent—and at a time when hourly wages were increased by a new labor contract.

About 60 workers were included in the program. They maintain aluminum reduction potlines that operate 24 hours a day. The company felt, however, that the necessary maintenance could be done by the day shift alone, working in five-day turns to provide coverage around the clock.

In changing over to the single shift, Kaiser considerably increased the degree of autonomy allowed the maintenance workers.

They are now allowed to bid on the type of work they prefer—either minor maintenance on the line or major rebuilding in the shop.

They work without supervision, set job priorities by their own judgment, and keep their own time records.

In addition to the cost savings brought about by reduced manpower requirements, potlines operated 99 percent of the time—a much better record than when maintenance was being handled on a "crash" basis.

Also, attitude interviews indicate that the workers developed closer feelings of identification with the company. For these reasons the program became a prototype for further job enrichment efforts throughout the plant.

**Productivity and Job Enrichment**

In many cases motivational causes of poor productivity are obvious. For example, a new plant of the Cryovac Division of W. R. Grace had trouble with quality and high production costs—even though the company had recruited and trained the best-qualified work force and supervisors in its history, and had put them all on salary instead of hourly wages.

Two facts made it seem likely that the plant's productivity problems were in motivation. First, the technology used was the most advanced available. Second, the plant started off with very high quality and productivity, which then dropped off. Apparently, neither advanced technology nor an attractive pay structure could assure continuing quality and productivity.

Sometimes collateral evidence of job dissatisfaction pinpoints problems of productivity as motivational. For example, at the Racine, Wisconsin, plant of Emerson Electric Co., a section that assembled trash compactors had problems with high costs and low quality. The indicators that motivational factors might be involved came from two statistics: absenteeism and turnover. They were higher in that department than the plant average.

At Kaiser Aluminum greater autonomy was the only significant change in the maintenance workers' jobs. Yet it was enough to cause considerable productivity improvement.

Frequently, granting additional authority to lower-level employees leads to ending distinctions between job categories. This occurred in the Cryovac plant. Before jobs were restructured, each production machine had a two-man team—an operator and an inspector-packer. The job redesign gave operators more responsibility at several crucial points where product quality was affected. As they took on this responsibility, it became possible to reduce the work force to one operator and two inspectors-packers for every two machines. Ultimately the distinction between the operator and the inspector-packer was eliminated. One man at one machine was able to perform both functions. Each man's job became more varied and interesting. The department realized a reduction of one-third in its manpower requirements.

### Job Enrichment and Feedback

Many unsuccessful job enrichment programs fail to accompany increased responsibility with *task feedback*—information about the effects of a worker's actions. The worker must learn how his actions affect other functions before he can exercise the self-control needed to live up to his increased responsibility.

In the data-processing division of a large insurance company, a high key-punch error rate led management to try job enrichment with a group of key-punch operators. One of the changes introduced to enrich jobs was designed specifically to increase feedback.

Under the old arrangement, operators never knew when they had made errors. All the cards they had punched were given to a supervisor, who sent them on to be processed for the computer. When the computer printout showed key-punch errors, the cards went back to the supervisor. Instead of returning incorrect cards to the operators who had made the errors, the supervisor gave them for correction to any operator who was not busy.

The new arrangement increased the autonomy of the operators in scheduling work, meeting deadlines, and deciding whether jobs had to be verified after punching. To provide feedback to complement this autonomy, the computer printout gave each operator a record of errors on every job. The operator set up a file of these printouts to determine for every job whether error rates increased or decreased. This kind of feedback motivates the operator to decrease the error rate.

A plant of Corning Glass Works in Massachusetts illustrates job enrichment in the context of organization development. In one assembly operation, laboratory hot plates are assembled from start to finish by a single worker, instead of moving through several work stations. Then the worker performs the inspection formerly done by another person. Thus he has immediate feedback on the quality of the product he has made.

At Emerson Electric Company, a strict assembly-line process was abandoned in favor of an assembly team. The team is identified on a label that is packed with the product assembled by the team. Any complaints from customers are sent to the team, whose members must draft a letter of reply.

These examples show how it is possible to improve feedback. Yet failure to do so is too common. As a result, job enrichment programs can fail to motivate, as they are supposed to do, and they can also lead to the production and quality problems that are characteristic of inadequate control.

**Starting a Job Enrichment Program**

There are six steps that used to be taken to install a successful job enrichment program:

1. *Data gathering and analysis.* The work group is studied in terms of working conditions, job attitudes, and work content.

2. *Education.* First, managers who might be affected by job enrichment are oriented on its general principles. Then the managers of the target work group receive basic training in motivational theory and job enrichment concepts. Finally, the work group managers meet to list all possible changes that might be made in the jobs in question.

3. *Primary implementation.* From the first list, the group managers pick the job changes that are practical and high in promise. They set priorities and resolve conflicts.

4. *Expanded implementation.* After trial on a few workers, the job changes are extended to others. The process of measuring results of the changes begins.

5. *Building autonomy.* Management of the job enrichment project is gradually passed from the consultant or internal specialist to line managers themselves.

6. *Final analysis.* Results are assessed, and responsibility for further action is fixed.

A typical job enrichment project takes about a year from the diagnostic phase through evaluation of results.

## Participative Management

Donnelly Mirrors Inc. of Holland, Michigan, employer of 600 persons, provides an example of participative management. Over several decades it has developed excellent employer-employee relationships. During this same period its productivity per employee has more than doubled. Profits have increased two and a half times. Absenteeism has declined to less than 1.5 percent. Labor turnover is about 6 percent a year; 97 percent of employees say they are satisfied with the company. Wages and benefits are tops in their area, and *all* employees participate in a monthly bonus.

The company attributes these results to trust, participation, tapping employee creativity and profit sharing.

Productivity bargaining for wages is a unique feature. All employees are paid a salary. An employees' committee decides what percentage increase will be asked and presents this percentage to management. Translated into dollars, this figure is increased by approximately 50 percent to get the amount of cost savings required. Thus, if the payroll were $3 million and the employees asked for a 10 percent raise:

| | |
|---|---|
| 10% of $3 million is | $300,000 |
| Add 50% | 150,000 |
| Total | $450,000 cost savings needed |

Forty percent of actual savings achieved goes into the bonus pool. Experience has shown pretty consistently that savings considerably *exceed* the required amount.

There probably is a limit to the economies which can be achieved by employee and supervisory ingenuity, but so far that limit has not been reached. The success of this company is likely an augury of the future.

## Production Teams

Some companies have set up partially autonomous teams of workers who are responsible for a tangible unit of production. Team members may perform a variety of tasks. Sometimes healthy competition among teams springs up. Some teams are temporary task forces including skilled workers from any department to tackle special one-time projects.

Goal setting and decision making are usually delegated to teams or task forces. When goals (time, cost, quantity, quality) are met, recognition and rewards are given. Advancement (money, status, jobs) is offered to persons who develop under the team system.

Productivity and quality then become the responsibility of every member of the group. Co-workers rather than superiors put pressure on lazy or careless workers. Peer pressure in teams reduces lateness and absenteeism especially if a group bonus is at stake.

In the team system the supervisor becomes a consultant. The team calls upon him when it can't meet its goals or runs into problems beyond the members' experience. Many groups set too-high goals. But team spirit and trying help them get more done than when the group doesn't stick together.

General Foods uses the team approach at its pet food plant to overcome employee boredom and loss of interest. Over several years' time each worker rotates from one major job to another. When he masters a new job, management increases his pay until he reaches the top rate. Employees are grouped into teams of about ten workers. The team leaders are similar to supervisors. But workers make production decisions in meetings of each group. The group takes responsibility for production, quality control, and maintenance. To increase team spirit, reserved parking spaces for management and time clocks have been eliminated. Group members decide when to take coffee breaks, and everyone eats in the same cafeteria.

The Questor Corporation, a diversified consumer-products company, has developed a successful program of participation at all levels, which is called "performance management." It includes five principal requirements. Employees must:

1. Be told clearly what specifically is expected of them.
2. Have the necessary knowledge and skill.
3. Be given feedback as to performance.
4. Be allotted the time, money, and equipment required.
5. Be "positively reinforced" (that is, paid fairly, recognized, allowed certain choices, provided opportunity to grow, and consulted in areas of competence).

Work groups solve their own problems—goals, assignments, troubleshooting, vacations, safety, quality, and the like. Supervisors teach, coach, and assist rather than boss. There are no time clocks; all employees are on salary. Involvement at all levels is the keynote of this program.

Similar experiments are being tried by General Electric, American Telephone and Telegraph, Polaroid, Texas Instruments, and Corning Glass. If these experiments solve some current employee relations problems, they will dramatically change orthodox management methods.

## The Demand for Participation

People the world over are demanding a greater voice in matters which affect their destiny. Consumer rebellion, citizen groups for better government, high turnover among middle managers, student demands, women's liberation, and union members' balking at the decisions of their officers are visible signs of their demands.

The desire of workers and managers for greater participation makes it easier to achieve involvement. Management by objectives, discussed later, is an example of greater involvement by all parties concerned. On the other hand, as autocratic authority diminishes, future managers will have more conflicting viewpoints to resolve as participation and involvement increase.

## The Results Approach in Personnel Practices

In personnel practices most employers react, rather than act. They wait until some need arises, then set up corrective measures.

Production, marketing, finance, and accounting functions are more carefully planned. Managers develop production scheduling, quality control, planned maintenance, market strategy, sales campaigns, cost finding, budgets, and similar planning and control methods.

Because employee relations are costly, they, too, deserve planning and control. These two management tools should be applied to selection, training, compensation, working conditions, employee health, fringe benefits, collective bargaining, and personnel research.

Applying a results approach to personnel practices requires standards of performance in each area. Here is a checklist to measure performance in personnel practices:

Percent labor turnover, annual basis.
Percent voluntary quits, annual basis.
Percent absenteeism, daily average.
Percent lateness, daily average.
Average age of the work force.
Average length of service.
Average hourly earnings, overtime.
Average hourly earnings, piece workers.
Average earnings in comparable jobs, other employers.
Lost time in accidents, duration in man-days, compensation costs.
Lost time due to strikes.
Test results—employment tests of abilities and interests, audiometer examinations, visual testing, physical examinations.
Noise studies; air temperature, humidity, and pollution; lighting; inspection of eating facilities.
Insurance claims—life, medical, hospitalization.
Retirement costs—funding and benefit payments.
Costs for employee recreation activities.
Performance appraisals and interviews.
Activities of credit union.
Suggestion system, awards.
Number of grievances.

Standards develop from the statistics gathered. Then, periodically new figures on personnel practices should be collected and measured against the standards. Change from the norms gives a control for personnel practices that is as helpful in planning as are controls used in the main functions of business.

It is true that many personnel activities are difficult to measure. Nevertheless, planning should specify expected results, whether quantitative or qualitative. Informed judgment should later be applied to results achieved to aid in future planning.

## The Concept of Personnel Accounting

In recent years, top managements have sought ways to measure the effectiveness of employee relations activities. The search is leading to a system of personnel accounting. Applying a results approach to personnel activities makes personnel accounting possible.

Here's an example. A $10,000 machine must return annually at minimum:

| | |
|---|---|
| $ 800 | (8% interest on the investment) |
| $1,000 | (full depreciation in ten years) |
| $1,000 | (10% pretax profit on capital) |
| $2,800 | |

Drawing a parallel, a $10,000 employee represents an investment, is subject to depreciation, and should contribute to profits.

Likewise, a personnel activity should justify its existence. Sometimes the justification can be expressed in numbers or dollars. Sometimes it must be the judgment of a superior about the achievement of planned goals. Some examples:

1. Employees complain about a muddy parking lot. Some turnover of personnel has resulted from it. How much money can management afford to invest to pave the lot?

2. The personnel department wants a full-time physician. Can the cost be justified financially?

3. The production manager asks for a company bus to carry employees from and to a low-income neighborhood. Is the expenditure wise?

So far there are no established human resources accounting (HRA) procedures. Some companies are experimenting with different approaches taking into account:

Hiring costs for various employee levels (debit).
Break-in costs until an employee becomes productive (debit).
Training costs beyond the break-in period (debit).
Labor turnover costs, including the above three (debit).
Absenteeism (debit).
Sickness—time lost (debit).
Accidents—time lost (debit).
Lateness, discipline (debit).
Compensation below or above the midpoint of grade (credit or debit).
Cost of handling grievances (debit).
Value of suggestions accepted (credit).
Strikes (debit).
Production above standard (credit).

Performance rating—below average (debit), above average (credit).
Length of service beyond break-in period (credit).
Promotion (credit).
Additional education (credit).

The values of debits and credits must be arbitrarily assigned. The HRA system should include office employees, supervisors, and hourly workers.

Under one plan the original credit for the whole work force is the annual payroll of those covered. At the end of the year this figure is modified by the debits and credits. Here's a hypothetical example.

Assume a million dollar payroll for 100 employees over the prior year:

| | *Debit* | *Credit* |
|---|---|---|
| Annual payroll, previous year | | $1,000,000 |
| Replacement of 25 employees | $ 7,500 | |
| Break-in costs, 25 employees | 5,000 | |
| Training costs beyond break-in | 8,000 | |
| Absenteeism | 5,000 | |
| Compensation, above midpoint | 6,000 | |
| Grievance handling | 1,500 | |
| Acceptance of suggestions | | 4,000 |
| Lateness, discipline | 1,000 | |
| Accidents, time lost | 4,000 | |
| Sickness, time lost | 5,000 | |
| Production, above standard | | 120,000 |
| Performance rating | | 5,000 |
| Length of service | | 50,000 |
| Promotions | | 4,000 |
| Additional education | | 2,000 |
| Civic activities | | 2,000 |
| Strikes | 0 | |
| Payroll, current year | 1,100,000 | |
| Totals | $1,143,000 | $1,187,000 |
| Gain | | 44,000 |

The years ahead should provide standards for a human resources accounting system. When perfected, it may become part of a company's annual report to stockholders. The gain might be considered increased value of human assets on the balance sheet or a contribution to profits on the profit and loss statement. If the Internal Revenue Service, stockholders, or the company comptroller objects to such unorthodox accounting procedures, separate calculations can be presented.

Stockholders expect management to account for the acquisition, maintenance, and productivity of its capital assets. Why not have a comparable accounting for the utilization of human assets?

## REVIEW

In your opinion, what are the advantages and disadvantages of the four-day work week?

What is flextime?

Differentiate job enlargement and job enrichment.

In applying a results approach to personnel practices, what measurements may be of use?

How would you define "personnel accounting"?

# 10

# DECISION-MAKING TECHNIQUES

"Don't just stand there, dammit! Make a decision!" That's what tactical officers shout at officer candidates in all the armed services. They believe, with justification, that *any decision* is better than *indecision*. Fortunately, business has developed techniques that are more helpful to managers than have been tactical officers' bellows to potential commanders.

Most managerial decisions are based on experience. However, from time to time a manager faces an important decision for which his experience provides no ready answer. Generally, the problem for which a decision is needed should be broken down into certain logical steps rather than judged as a whole. The sequence of these steps is (1) defining the problem, (2) gathering information, (3) selecting the most feasible solution, and (4) carrying out the decision.

## Defining the Problem

Charles Kettering, famous scientist and inventor, once said, "A problem well stated is a problem half solved." The right questions must be asked. This requirement means digging deeper than surface symptoms. The problem needs to be analyzed, not just accepted as something to be overcome. For example, management may think that its problem is to reduce production costs. But the real problem may be how to get salesmen to sell profitable products rather than to push easily sold, low-profit items.

Many important decisions are concerned with allocating relatively scarce resources—money, materials, skills, specialized knowledge, space, time, or energy. Short-term profits or long-term growth may call for different choices.

Here are some questions which may help in clarifying the true nature of a problem:

- ☐ Is this problem financial, material or human?
- ☐ Has it ever been encountered before?
- ☐ Are there policies, precedents, or practices which have helped to solve this problem in the past?
- ☐ What additional sources should be explored?
- ☐ What facilities do we have which can contribute?

In our fast-changing environment some decisions are unique. They have not been made before and so no precedents exist. Therefore, executive decision making needs high-level understanding, vision, and courage.

There is no single "decision theory." Instead, there are various techniques, devices, and viewpoints for weighing possible courses of action. All are designed to increase fact gathering and decrease risk.

Managers often discover that solving one problem causes new ones. Examples:

1. A company which changed to the four-day week found an increase in alcoholism.

2. Many companies which set up mechanized assembly lines have suffered increased absenteeism.

3. A few companies with job enrichment programs report more anxiety among some employees.

4. Setting up a central typing pool in a utility company caused idleness among high-level executive secretaries.

5. Inventory controls increased production at lower costs in a paper company but resulted in customer dissatisfaction.

Sensible managers consider possible repercussions when deciding how problems have to be solved.

Defining the problem also includes deciding how to find a solution. Choices include ignoring the problem, deferring a decision, deciding on the basis of hunch or experience, extensive discussion, brainstorming, applying an accepted principle (deduction), relying on staff specialists, or hiring outside consultants. The procedures used to find a solution may include review of existing literature, trial and error, controlled experimentation, data compilation (leading to inductive conclusions), graphic presentations, models, statistical analyses, mathematical simulation, and computerized solutions.

The approach to a financial or material problem differs from that used with a people-oriented problem. The latter involves the nature of the work, formal relations, reporting responsibilities, authorities, use of staff, policies, kind of supervision, and budgetary constraints. Moreover, the informal organization may also have bearing: norms of group behavior, communication, conflicting ambitions, and status rankings.

## Gathering Information

The importance of a decision should determine how much pertinent information will be gathered. There are three general types:

1. Measurements—capacities, quantities, costs. Example: "The machine at maximum produces 1800 units per hour."
2. Facts—historical, descriptive. Example: "The Occupational Safety and Health Act (OSHA) is now being vigorously enforced."
3. Opinions. Example: "All three companies visited were enthusiastic about this equipment."

There are external and internal information sources. External sources consist of the following:

*Environment*—social, political, legal, local, ecological, etc.

*Economy*—trends, forecasts, correlations, data on present status, rates of interest, etc.

*Competition*—products, companies, territories, extent, probable plans, etc.

Internal sources are:

*Financial*—capital, manufacturing, marketing, inventory, profits, etc.

*Nonfinancial*—organization, personnel, methods, facilities, research, etc.

The organization of material is important. At this point the right questions must be asked. For example, one company decided to build a plant for producing a new product. The question asked was where the plant should be located. Data were accumulated, a decision was made, and the plant was built. After three years of unprofitable operation, it was sold. The right question should have been not where but *whether* a new plant should be built.

Information gathered should be graded as to importance: D, discard; R, retain; U, useful; I, important. Likewise, assumptions should be graded as to percent likelihood of correctness.

## Selecting the Most Feasible Solution

Management sometimes picks a solution that's not ideal but may be the best under existing conditions. Perhaps a company would prefer to replace equipment bought some years earlier but not fully paid for, with new, costly equipment. The new machinery might be the ideal answer, but the best decision at this time might be to get sales volume that will keep the old equipment running at capacity.

When selecting a solution, management has to take into account comparative expenses or capital costs of other solutions. Time factors such as deadlines, time required for equipment delivery or plant construction, and the present phase of the business cycle must be considered. Management must also consider the capabilities of personnel available to carry out the decision. And the risks of each choice have to be weighed against expected benefits.

Historically, mathematics has played an important part in managerial decision making. Double-entry bookkeeping, accounting, cost finding, marginal analysis, break-even analysis, overhead distribution, budgeting, and other arithmetic means have helped managers make decisions.

In recent years more sophisticated mathematics has been used, such as statistical analyses—averages, ratios, deviations, errors, correlation, regressions; time series—secular trends, cyclical variations, seasonal fluctuations, index numbers; extrapolation of data; curves of first, second, and third degree and other contours.

Linear programming, game theory, probabilities, mathematical models, optimization, econometrics, and other highly sophisticated applications of higher mathematics require the use of computers. Linear programming, for example, has been used to determine the best location for a plant, optimum plant size, best product mix, economic inventory size, and the most efficient channels of distribution.

The manager who is not familiar with these mathematical techniques can frequently use charts to bolster his judgment. A bar chart can compare quantities. A curve that reflects past events can show a trend with variations. Plottings at coordinated intersections on a scatter diagram can indicate correlation, or even predict an unknown variable from a known one. Ratio charts, plotted on semilogarithmic scales, can compare changes in two variables of quite different magnitudes.

A manager who does not use either a mathematical or graphic approach can sometimes use samples or controlled experiments. This approach is frequently used by sales managers in estimating the reception of a new product in a test market.

## Carrying Out the Decision: The Decision Tree

One interesting technique to assist in executive decision making is the *decision tree*. It diagrams alternatives and subdivides them as shown in Figure 15. Here's the story behind this diagram.

The owner of the Nuline Furniture Company died. He was insured in favor of the company for $1 million. His three sons, who were active in the business, soon disagreed over which was the best way to use the proceeds of the insurance policy.

Tom, vice president of manufacturing, wanted to further mechanize production. Dick, vice president of sales, thought the money should be used to develop and merchandise a new, low-priced line of furniture for apartment dwellers. Harry, the treasurer, feared an economic recession and suggested investing the money at 8 or 9 percent interest for the time being.

Each brother gathered accounting and other data to support his position. After weeks of discussion, they still had these three possibilities of using the money:

*Proposal A—Further Mechanization.* This discussion covered conveyorization and/or a comprehensive industrial engineering survey, with a final implementing program. Estimates were made of

*Figure 15. Decision tree presentation.*

| Decision Tree | | | | Percent ROI first year | Percent ROI fifth year | Comments |
|---|---|---|---|---|---|---|
| $1,000,000 to invest | A Further mechanization | D Conveyor system | H Overhead conveyors $1,000,000 | 5% | 12% | Possible 20% production increase. Develop details. |
| | | | I Movable roller conveyors, plus new warehouse | 3% | 7% | Discard. Inferior to "H" above. |
| | | E Industrial engineering consultant | J Estimated fee $200,000 | 0% | 9% | Discard. Fee exorbitant. No assurance of success. |
| | | | K Implementing program $800,000 | 6% | 9% | Discard because "J" was discarded. |
| | B New products | F New line of apartment furniture | L If first-year sales $500,000 | 10% | 12% | Discard. Existing plant could not add this much production. New plant too risky. |
| | | | M If first-year sales $100,000 | –10% | 4% | Discard. Unprofitable. |
| | | G Market research for new items | N Budgeted cost $200,000 | 0% | 10% | Defer. Look to future by promoting trained salesman to full-time market researcher. |
| | | | O Produce new items $800,000 | 6% | 10% | |
| | C Investment at interest | | P Buy AAA bonds | 6% | 6%? | Discard. Inflation could reduce purchasing power of such a safe but low return. |
| | | | Q Buy up company stock | 9% | 10% + | Discard. Would benefit brothers and their mother – but additional taxes too high. |
| | | | R Buy commercial paper | 9.5% | 9.5% | Discard. Good idea now, but higher prices for equipment probable in the future. |

production increases, reductions in labor, overtime, and fringe benefit costs. Added sales, clerical, and shipping costs for an expected 20 percent increase in output were calculated. Storage, depreciation, production scheduling, equipment maintenance, and other problems were projected.

*Proposal B—New Products.* Vice president Dick continued presenting his idea of a low-priced furniture line for apartment dwellers. His brothers agreed that market research might prove or disprove Dick's proposal, or come up with other new product ideas. They agreed on probable sales volumes, gross profit, sales promotion, additions to sales force and selling expenses. However, a new line, if successful, might require a second shift, in an already tight labor market.

*Proposal C—Invest the Money.* Harry pointed out that this approach allowed time to determine whether an economic recession might occur. 90-day commercial paper could yield 8 percent. Longer commitments might yield 9 percent, which was about what the company made on its invested capital. Nuline had plenty of working capital. By keeping the money available, Harry thought, Nuline might be able to buy controlling interest in one of its competitors if a recession occurred. Tom commented that if there was no recession, but continuing inflation, the purchasing power of the $1 million would shrink.

In this impasse, they finally called in a financial consultant. Here are the steps he took.

First, he studied the data assembled by each brother, to spell out investment costs, time factors, space implications, and other ramifications. Working with the comptroller, he computed the return on investment (ROI) of the most likely alternatives.

(Each alternative would require an investment of money to be put into practice. After an alternative has been put into practice, hopefully the result will be a profit. Subtracting the investment from the profit made during five years, for example, would provide a five-year return on investment. Divide this figure by the amount of the investment, then multiply by 100, and divide the result by five. Now you have the annual percent ROI. Of course, an actual calculation of ROI is more complicated than this, as is shown in the next section.)

Then the consultant and the three brothers developed the decision tree shown in Figure 15 on the left, and the reasoning used, shown at the right of the decision tree. As a result, they reduced the choices to H, to install overhead conveyors, or Q, to buy up their company stock, the price of which was then depressed. However, their income tax accountant showed that if they used the $1 million to buy up their stock, each brother and their mother would retain little of the increased dividends that would result. For that reason, H got the final vote.

There are three major benefits of using the decision tree technique for making decisions:

*Conflict reduction.* Often, a major company decision has the potential of affecting the careers and ambitions of some executives adversely, while others stand to gain considerably. The decision tree technique takes emotion and personal interest out of such a situation and brings the executive team together.

*Systematized thinking.* The decision tree technique pins down the logical order of outcomes resulting if the various alternatives were to be put into practice. This makes it fairly easy to compare the advantages and disadvantages of each alternative.

*Making the best decision.* The decision tree technique permits the most promising decision to be made with confidence for two reasons: (1) Alternatives are easily weighed against each other, especially with the help of mathematical comparisons of ROI and risk factors. (The risk factor of an alternative is the estimated percentage of probability that the alternative will occur. Risk factors are usually part of very complex decision tree presentations.) (2) Subjective feelings have no place in the decision tree technique.

## Return on Investment

Top management must always be concerned with what kind of return any proposed investment may bring. And the bank or other institution that is asked to finance a new investment will be equally interested in the return expected from it.

In the long run, the success of a management is largely the long-range effect of its capital investment decisions. Many management decisions, such as personnel, selling, and organization structure, can be reversed or modified more easily than those which result in heavy investment in land, buildings, and equipment.

Since the supply of capital funds is limited, a management must decide from a number of alternatives just how new capital will be used. The intelligent way to make this decision is to estimate the likely return on investment (ROI) from each alternative and then to compare those estimates to find the most promising one.

Estimating ROI can involve simple computations, or extremely complex ones, depending on how many factors and assumptions are used. Here are the principal factors, defined in simple terms:

*Original investment.* Actual cost of the investment (in a new machine, for example) at time of purchase, after any allowable discounts.

*Net investment.* Original investment, plus installation expenses, plus or minus any change in *working* capital caused by the new investment, minus trade-in and/or expected salvage value.

*Salvage value.* Money received for sale of old investment, or for trade-in. It may be actual or anticipated, and should be treated as a deduction from the original investment, not as income. Typically the curve of salvage value is a declining, decelerating one, with the greatest drop occurring the first year.

*Cash income.* Net income after tax which can be credited to the new machine, plus compound interest earned or earnable on each year's net income if that income is invested. The rate of interest should be based on past experience of the company, not on the rate expected from any proposed investments. In simpler computations some managers use merely projected labor plus material savings due to the new machine.

*Depreciation.* Decline in value of a tangible asset due to use or passage of time.

*Obsolescence.* Decline in value of a tangible asset due to changed conditions, technological improvements, cessation of demand, style changes, adverse legislation, or other influences which cause tangible assets to cease to be useful or profitable. It is a hazardous assumption.

*Economic life.* The period of time over which cash income (or prime cost savings) from the investment can reasonably be expected, before replacement or capital additions will become necessary.

*Maintenance expense.* Cost of repairs and servicing which can be charged off as current expense and hence are not classed as capital additions.

In the past, managers used "time to get your money back" as the sole criterion of a proposed capital investment. Thus, if a machine costs $12,000 and yields annual savings of $3,000, the time would be four years. A somewhat better approach is given in the following example, which is based on estimated labor and material savings only. This very simple procedure ignores compound interest, depreciation, obsolescence, added working capital needed, costs of maintenance, and other refinements.

| | |
|---|---|
| Labor and material savings per year | $ 3,000 |
| Multiplied by 10 years of useful life (estimated) | 30,000 |
| Less net investment (as defined above) | 12,000 |
| Return | $18,000 |
| Divided by net investment × 100 | 150 |
| Divided by years of useful life to yield annual return on investment | 15% |

Professionals in the financial field will turn up their noses at these calculations, which could scarcely be claimed to provide a true return on investment. They are, however, better than the "years to get your money back" approach.

Here's a more sophisticated example of the calculations for the first five years' life of a new machine.

| | | |
|---|---|---|
| Original investment (cost of new machine) | $60,000 | |
| Plus installation cost (capital charge) | 10,000 | |
| Plus additional working capital needed | 20.000 | |
| 5-year loan needed | | $90,000 |
| Interest on loan @ 7%: $6,300/year | | |
| Minus salvage value (estimated), end of 5 years | | 15,000 |
| Net investment | | $75,000 |

The company now earns 8 percent interest on each year's invested net income.

Anticipated net income, after tax, from the new machine:

| *Year* | *Net Income* | | *8% Interest* | |
|---|---|---|---|---|
| 1 | $ 40,000 | | — | |
| 2 | 40,000 | | $ 3,200 | |
| 3 | 40,000 | | 6,400 | |
| 4 | 40,000 | | 9,600 | |
| 5 | 40,000 | | 12,800 | |
| Cash income: | $200,000 | plus | $32,000 | equals $232,000 |

| | | |
|---|---|---|
| Interest on loan ($6,300 × 5 years) | $31,500 | |
| Plus loan principal | 90,000 | |
| Minus expenses | | 121,500 |
| 5-year return on investment | | $110,500 |
| 5-year percent return on investment | $\frac{\$110{,}500}{\$\ 75{,}000} \times 100$ | 147.3% |
| Annual percent return on investment | $\frac{147.3}{5 \text{ years}}$ | 29.5% |

In addition, there is $35,000 accumulated in depreciation reserves (straight-line depreciation of 10 percent per year over five years on the $70,000 investment, that is, cost of installed machine). Moreover, the depreciated machine, which currently has a salvage value of $15,000 and a remaining life of five. years, continues in use.

Perfectionists in the ROI field will point out that many elements are missing from these calculations—discounted money, value of compound interest on the interest at 8 percent, inflation, cost of maintenance, probable inadequacy of the accumulated depreciation reserves to purchase new equipment at the end of ten years, return after the period of full depreciation, corporate income tax, probable technological obsolescence of the machine before ten years, and other factors. But the computations will give an idea as to the assumptions which must be made and the complexity of the problem as more and more factors are taken into account.

One sophisticated way to compare the merits of two proposed uses of capital is to calculate the present value of the calculated return over the useful life of each investment.

So many assumptions must be made in the more refined methods of calculating ROI that there is much to be said for simpler formulas. Since each problem is unique, no single formula exists; the factors and assumptions to be considered must be judged on the importance of the problem, the data available, and the mathematical expertise of those responsible for the study.

## The Business Cycle and Capital Investment

Business cycles of most developed nations usually have durations of three and a half years, 60 percent of that time showing a rise, 40 percent a decline. However, cycles from one industry to another may differ and in some cases are considerably longer than three and a half years.

Some capital investment decisions can be implemented within a few months. Others, such as a new plant, may require two or three years. Many capital investment decisions must be made when the cycle is swinging downward. Most managers would prefer to wait until the business outlook seems excellent before committing themselves to capital investments. But this point may be far along in the business upturn. As a result, the construction may be completed or the new machinery installed about the time that a downswing is under way. So capital investment decisions are often psychologically hard to make.

Here is a method to judge where the economy stands in the current business cycle:

1. Select one index which is representative of the industry.
2. Secure monthly data for the last three business cycles, possibly 12 to 15 years.
3. Compute and plot on graph paper a 12-month moving average for this period, thereby eliminating seasonal fluctuations. If the resulting curve shows a clear business cycle, study the average duration in months. Study the amplitude, that is, the average width from low to high. Estimate where in the current cycle the business now stands.
4. Estimate the probable time for a proposed investment to come on line. This can give the manager ammunition to support his commitment to the investment decision. Business cycles do in-

fluence capital spending. Knowing what phase of its cycle the industry is in helps the decision-making process.

## Importance of Company Records

In many decisions, company records play a vital part. The creation, duplication, distribution, storage, availability, and ultimate disposition of records involve considerable expense. The computer has changed the nature of many records but has not reduced the volume.

Planning includes studies of record creation—size, copies, standards, paper, magnetic tape, disk pack, method of production, distribution. Control includes storage after use, retrieval methods, and an orderly program of disposition. Handling of transaction records (invoices, checks, correspondence, etc.) is usually easier than storage and retrieval of reference material (legal items, reports, research, brochures, etc.).

The records manager is far above the file clerk level. Usually this manager can advise but not decide on necessity of production or use of records. Records management is a service function. Data processing and records management work closely together. One of the primary sources of information for decision making lies in company records.

## Control Systems

A decision is static until translated into action. The decision itself sets the ultimate goal, but it may have to be divided into subgoals, with time limits and responsibility designated for each part.

Control systems include coordination to insure that each person makes his contribution on time. Additionally control systems avoid diluting, misinterpreting, and slowing down the program as it passes down to lower organization levels.

Figure 16 shows a simple planning and control device. The chart resulted from the decision of an eastern seaboard company to undertake national distribution over a five-year period.

A Critical Path network such as illustrated in Figure 9 could have been used instead of the easily constructed chart shown in Figure 16. Whatever control device is used, close follow-up is essential if an important decision is to have a profitable result.

*Figure 16. Planning and control device for a marketing division.*

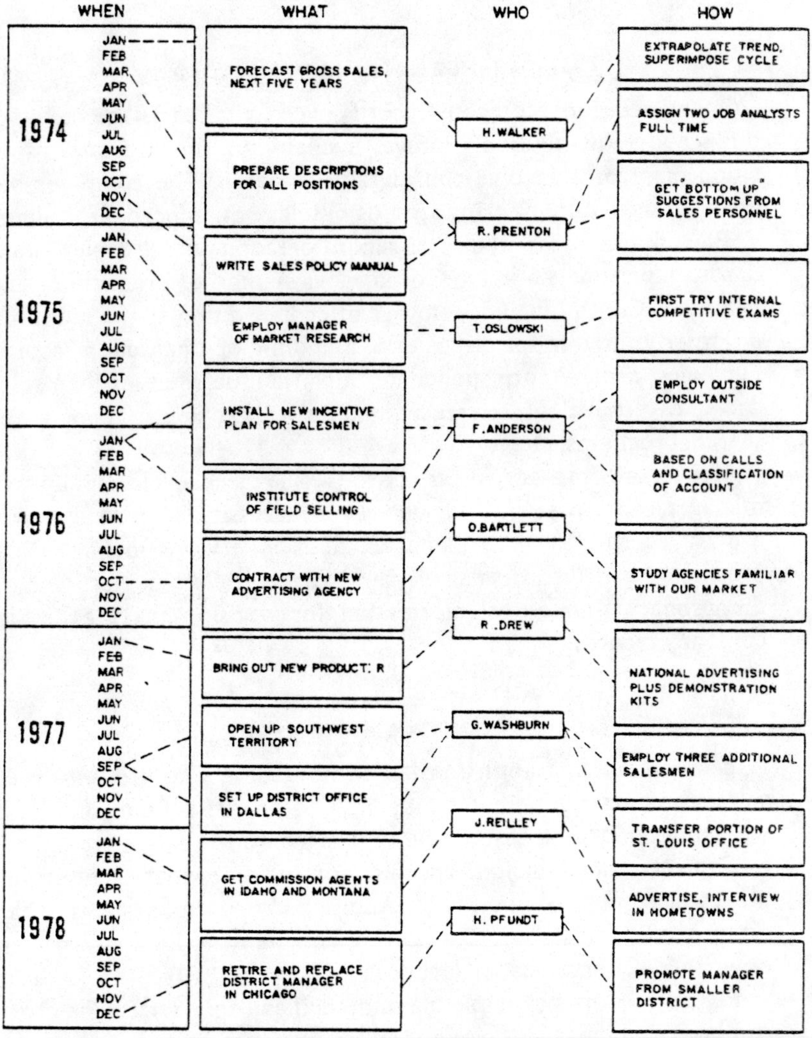

WHEN

1974
JAN
FEB
MAR
APR
MAY
JUN
JUL
AUG
SEP
OCT
NOV
DEC

1975
JAN
FEB
MAR
APR
MAY
JUN
JUL
AUG
SEP
OCT
NOV
DEC

1976
JAN
FEB
MAR
APR
MAY
JUN
JUL
AUG
SEP
OCT
NOV
DEC

1977
JAN
FEB
MAR
APR
MAY
JUN
JUL
AUG
SEP
OCT
NOV
DEC

1978
JAN
FEB
MAR
APR
MAY
JUN
JUL
AUG
SEP
OCT
NOV
DEC

WHAT

FORECAST GROSS SALES, NEXT FIVE YEARS

PREPARE DESCRIPTIONS FOR ALL POSITIONS

WRITE SALES POLICY MANUAL

EMPLOY MANAGER OF MARKET RESEARCH

INSTALL NEW INCENTIVE PLAN FOR SALESMEN

INSTITUTE CONTROL OF FIELD SELLING

CONTRACT WITH NEW ADVERTISING AGENCY

BRING OUT NEW PRODUCT: R

OPEN UP SOUTHWEST TERRITORY

SET UP DISTRICT OFFICE IN DALLAS

GET COMMISSION AGENTS IN IDAHO AND MONTANA

RETIRE AND REPLACE DISTRICT MANAGER IN CHICAGO

WHO

H. WALKER

R. PRENTON

T. OSLOWSKI

F. ANDERSON

O. BARTLETT

R. DREW

G. WASHBURN

J. REILLEY

H. PFUNDT

HOW

EXTRAPOLATE TREND, SUPERIMPOSE CYCLE

ASSIGN TWO JOB ANALYSTS FULL TIME

GET "BOTTOM UP" SUGGESTIONS FROM SALES PERSONNEL

FIRST TRY INTERNAL COMPETITIVE EXAMS

EMPLOY OUTSIDE CONSULTANT

BASED ON CALLS AND CLASSIFICATION OF ACCOUNT

STUDY AGENCIES FAMILIAR WITH OUR MARKET

NATIONAL ADVERTISING PLUS DEMONSTRATION KITS

EMPLOY THREE ADDITIONAL SALESMEN

TRANSFER PORTION OF ST. LOUIS OFFICE

ADVERTISE, INTERVIEW IN HOMETOWNS

PROMOTE MANAGER FROM SMALLER DISTRICT

## REVIEW

What major steps are usually followed in making an important, unique decision?

Name some useful procedures which can be utilized.

Name three kinds of information which may be needed.

Sketch a decision tree for some important decision you have made.

Name the principal items to be considered in calculating return on investment.

What is records management?

# 11

# THE ART OF DELEGATION

"The only way I can get the job done right is to do it myself." That's a complaint heard too often among managers. The "do it myself" managers are confessing failure in a crucial managerial talent, the art of delegation.

Don't confuse the terms "decentralization" and "delegation." By decentralization, management extends authority and responsibility to lower *organization levels*. It is a process. Delegation transfers responsibilities with commensurate authority to *subordinates*. It is an act. "Decentralization," a process, is a larger term than "delegation," an act.

## Decentralization

So much has been written about decentralization that many managers think it's the only way to organize. This conclusion is not necessarily true. In fact, some well-known companies are recentralizing portions of their organizations. Whether decentralization is called for depends on what results it's expected to achieve.

The factors that bring on decentralization include easing the burden on top executives, diversification of products, market emphasis, distance and transportation, manager development, and motivation improvement.

The three major forms of organization—functional, geographic, and divisional—are not by themselves decentralization. Unless authority and responsibility are pushed down to lower organization levels, decentralization doesn't occur.

Some activities, policies or decisions can be handled better from headquarters than from a decentralized geographic region. For example, one company was able to disperse inventories by setting up local warehouses. Controls of inventory and purchasing were centralized by feeding data from warehouse terminals into the company's headquarters computer.

Decentralization of a company might hurt, rather than help develop, a regional manager. The policies and decisions he makes can be different from those made in other regions, but it could be unsafe for them to conflict with those of other regions.

There is a sequence for effectively decentralizing a company. The sequence includes determining appropriate *centralization* of certain activities, development of managers, provisions for communication, coordination of the decentralized units, and development of controls. Only then should the activities to be dispersed be decided upon.

The profit center is one concept of decentralization. Each center sets up a kind of integrated, self-contained business within the management framework as a whole. It has its own management group and its own staff support and is virtually set up in business on a competitive basis, accounting-wise.

## Delegation

When a manager delegates, he transfers responsibilities to a subordinate. Those responsibilities include authority to act. The manager and the subordinate agree upon standards of performance and accountability.

Figure 17 illustrates delegation graphically. Here a manager has delegated responsibility for performance of certain physical, mental, and social duties with corresponding authority, that is, control over the necessary human, material, and financial resources. The circle is not complete, however, without accountability for the discharge of the responsibility and exercise of authority. This accountability feeds back to the delegating manager.

*Figure 17. Circle of delegation.*

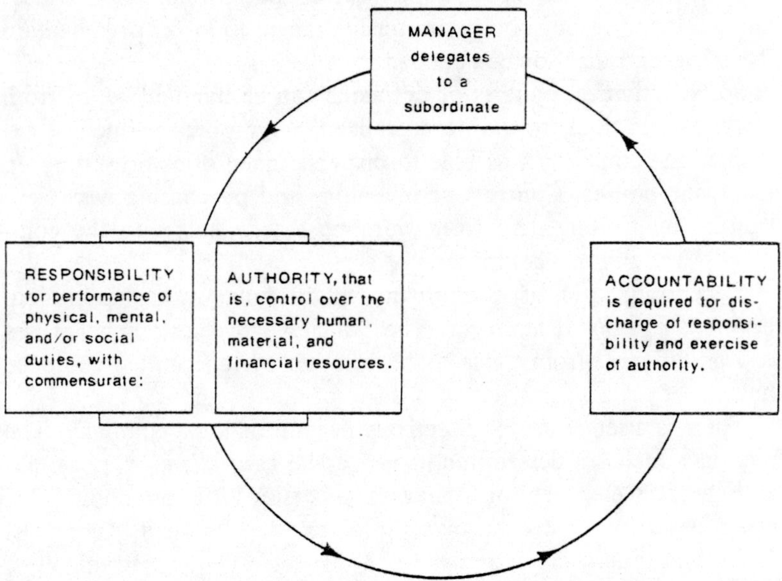


In theory, at least, a manager could delegate all his responsibilities and all his authority to subordinates. But the manager cannot delegate his own accountability to a higher authority. He would be held accountable for delegating all his responsibilities and authorities and therefore for all actions of his subordinates.

Why delegate? Managers are relieved of small, time-consuming routine details which can be adequately performed by subordinates. This frees higher-level managers for larger responsibilities. Many times, better decisions can be made at lower levels closer to where the action is. Delegation helps subordinates develop new skills and prepares them for promotion. Broader scope and diversity encourage new ideas from subordinates and improve morale.

Disadvantages of delegation may include less uniformity, duplication of staff functions, conflict, and poor and costly decisions. These disadvantages simply mean that management has not done its job in selection, training, and development of personnel. Of course, there are risks in delegation, but the benefits more than offset them.

**How to Delegate**

Here are five suggestions on how to delegate:

1. Make a written job analysis. Fill in a large sheet such as shown in Figure 18. Enter in each column the high-, average-, and low-level duties of each present responsibility. List authorities to employ personnel, purchase materials, change methods, and the like, in the spaces provided. This sheet analyzes job duties and authorities but not how to get the job done.

2. Decide which duties and authorities of the job are to be delegated. The authorities must be adequate for performance of the duties delegated. Make either a horizontal cut across the job analysis sheet to delegate a group of lower-level duties, or a vertical cut to delegate all levels of a single duty.

*Figure 18. Job analysis for delegation.*

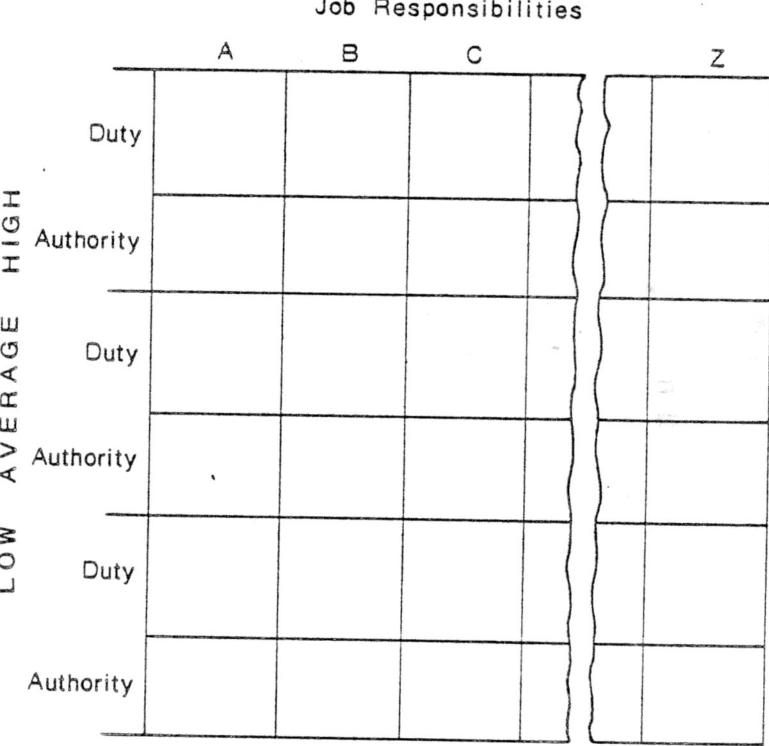

3. Next explain the duties and authorities being delegated to the person who will handle them. Establish standards of performance with his agreement. Also explain his accountability for performance. This constitutes control on his execution of new duties.

4. Give him a few days to think about what's being delegated and then ask him to explain his concept of it. Review and correct any misconceptions.

5. Periodically review or check his understanding and performance of the delegated duties. Give noncritical coaching for any errors or misunderstanding. Help him acquire needed skills. Give praise and financial recognition for progress and accomplishment.

Subordinates generally feel their superiors do not delegate enough. This attitude is particularly true of technical men. Managers fail to delegate for various reasons. Some doubt that subordinates are capable enough, intelligent enough, or have enough experience. Others feel subordinates lack ambition and personality.

Sometimes managers are afraid that subordinates might prove more capable than themselves. Managers past their prime or faced with new technology are likely candidates for this fear. Sometimes assistant managers understand problems better than their bosses, so the bosses' decisions simply frustrate them.

In some cases managers fear that delegation lessens their own importance. They know they can't handle more important duties. Having carved out their own little empires, they defend them vigorously and resist delegating.

In many instances a manager has not analyzed his own job, so he doesn't know what should be delegated. He may also have failed to analyze the abilities of his subordinates and therefore may not know who can accept delegation.

Not all delegation is downward from superior to subordinate. It may also be lateral. Activities once considered line have been turned over to staff departments such as purchasing, employee relations, quality control, market research, new product development, and others. Sometimes these staff units report to line authority but at other times they are completely divorced from it.

Many top managers preach delegation to their subordinates without practicing it themselves. When any manager makes a job analysis like that illustrated in Figure 17, he will learn how many delegable duties he is performing. This realization alone can cause some managers to delegate. Sometimes loading a manager with new activities forces him to strip himself of some of his present duties. For an ambitious manager, the mere prospect of promotion to a higher job can often be enough to start him delegating. Management performance appraisals take into account how well managers have delegated. Some companies hold group discussions with managers on why and how to delegate. Such discussions among managers stimulate delegating.

In addition to delegation by managers, many scientists, engineers, and technical specialists perform low-level tasks which could easily be delegated to assistants, draftsmen, laboratory helpers, maintenance men or clerks.

### Authorities

One of the most puzzling and difficult parts of delegation is the delegation of authority. The term "authority" is so nebulous that it is necessary to make it more specific. For example, authority to approve, to authorize, or to take action represents three degrees. Generally, the higher the level of management, the fewer the limitations on authority. However, it's desirable to stipulate conditions or limits of the authority. The following list gives some delegated authorities with typical limitations. In most of the items listed, the authority can be to approve, to authorize, or to act.

**TYPICAL AUTHORITIES**

| Kind of Authority | Conditions or Limitations |
|---|---|
| Capital Items | |
| Purchase equipment | Up to \$ 1,000 |
| Purchase property | Up to \$15,000 |
| Sell property | Up to \$ 5,000 |
| Expense Items | |
| Hotel and travel | Provided receipts are submitted. |
| Entertainment | If dates and names of guests are submitted with receipts. |
| Moving (household) | For present employees only. |
| Dues | In trade associations and technical societies only. |

| | |
|---|---|
| Gifts or donations | Up to $100. |
| Employee group activities | Within budget allowance. |
| Petty cash | Under $10 if supported by requisition or receipts. |
| Purchases | Under $100 if initiated by a numbered requisition. |
| Contracts | For routine services. |
| Consulting services | Maximum $4,000 fee per month to any one consulting firm. Excludes legal, auditing, and engineering. |
| Maintenance and repair | Routine maintenance of buildings, land, and equipment. |
| Employees | |
| Hire employees | If replacements and at no higher salary. |
| Hire additional employees | Up to $70 salary per month. |
| Hire temporary employees | For maximum of three months. |
| Discharge employees | From his department only. |
| Promote employees | To existing vacant job. |
| Grant wage or salary increases | Authorized under the job evaluation plan. |
| Sign labor contracts | Within limits established by board of directors. |
| Overtime pay | Up to 16 hours a week for any one employee. |
| Pay for absence | Under schedule in supervisors' manual. |
| Sales | |
| Advertising and sales promotion | Within limit of 2% of gross sales. |
| Prices | As shown in price list; may allow 10% discount for quantity. |
| Credit | Any amount or terms, unless previously restricted by credit department. |
| Acceptance of orders | Concurrence of production department for unusual specifications or deliveries. |

Delegation should be put in writing. The specific responsibilities, the limits of authority, the standards to be met, and the manner of accountability should all be spelled out in a job description. Putting it in writing reduces misunderstanding.

## THE EXCEPTION PRINCIPLE

The exception principle requires that only exceptions to standard data be brought to the attention of the responsible manager. For example, each month a computer produces 90 sheets of sales analysis data, by territory, salesmen, customers, products cumulative to date, comparisons with the same period last year and last month. The busy sales manager cannot digest all this data. Here's how he can use the exception principle:

- ☐ He establishes high and low standards for monthly sales by territory, salesman, customer, and product. An assistant reviews the data and marks with a blue pencil figures above the standard, with a red pencil figures below the standard. The sales manager quickly spots these exceptions and then takes action.
- ☐ The computer can be programmed so that it will only print out data below or above the standards.

Management by exception saves executive time and results in quicker action. The executive who uses the exception principle is delegating to his subordinates the authority to handle routine matters. Only the exceptions to the standards he has set are brought to his attention.

## MANAGEMENT BY OBJECTIVES

Management by objectives (MBO) can be defined as "management by results rather than by activities." Specific goals become the concern of every manager. Delegating becomes an integral part of managing when MBO is used. MBO cannot succeed without delegation at all organization levels.

Advocates of MBO have applied the concept to different situations in industry, commerce, public service, education, and other organized efforts. MBO has, at least, these eight basic ground rules:

1. Individual and group goals support organization objectives.
2. Managers, staff specialists, and key employees participate in setting job objectives.
3. Objectives are specific, attainable, and measurable in units, costs, ratios, percentages, time, etc.

4. Standards of performance are agreed upon by the job holder and his superior.
5. Self-imposed objectives and standards have the greatest motivation.
6. Responsibilities, authorities, and activities are aimed at specific objectives.
7. Feedback and recognition for outstanding work are necessary.
8. Job objectives must be reviewed regularly and revised when job content is changed.

For MBO to work, goals must be set at all levels, from the highest on down. Top management must be totally committed to the MBO program or it will fail. Results must be appraised. While most companies set objectives at various levels, this is only one step in MBO, though an important one.

MBO is not just another management technique. It is a new way of managing. If objectives at all levels can be clearly seen, a company can stay on course by concentrating on the agreed-upon goals. In goal setting, planning, organizing, coordinating, and controlling, MBO must take into account the abilities, attitudes, expectations, and participation of the members of the management team.

Objectives particularly must be carefully evaluated. They must be important, challenging, specific, and attainable within some definite period of time. High achievers are more motivated by such goals than low or average achievers. Since most employees will follow a strongly motivated leader, it pays to identify the high achievers. For them, money is not the incentive to effort but rather a measure of success; *achievement* is the real incentive.

### Activities versus Objectives

MBO puts the accent on objectives rather than performance of activities. To make the distinction clear, the following lists give some examples of typical activities and objectives.

## TYPICAL ACTIVITIES

General Supervisory

| | |
|---|---|
| Selects capable employees | Recommends wage or salary increases |
| Trains employees | Improves work procedures |
| Conducts meetings | Submits accurate reports on time |
| Plans work daily | |

Manufacturing

Eliminates safety hazards
Insures supplies on hand
Ensures condition of tools and equipment
Inspects incoming materials
Inspects outgoing work

Marketing

Conducts market research
Devises compensation plans for salesmen
Conducts sales contests
Takes telephone orders
Solicits sales
Prepares advertising and sales promotion material

Office

Figures costs
Handles purchasing
Dictates letters
Operates office machines
Prepares budgets

Engineering

Prepares specifications
Analyzes bids
Designs products
Designs equipment

## TYPICAL OBJECTIVES

### Manufacturing

Increase production by $x\%$ per man-hour
Reduce labor cost by $x\%$ per unit
Reduce manufacturing cost by $x\%$ per sales dollar
Reduce manufacturing overhead on prime costs by $x\%$
Increase productive machine hours by $x\%$
Reduce waste by $x\%$
Reduce overtime by $x\%$
Reduce man-days lost through accidents by $x\%$
Reduce rejects by $x\%$
Reduce machine downtime by $x\%$

### Marketing

Increase dollar sales by $x\%$
Increase the more profitable items by $x\%$
Increase sales by $x\%$
Eliminate unprofitable customers
Eliminate unprofitable items
Redesign products
Find new products
Increase advertising inquiries by $x\%$
Decrease sales expenses by $x\%$ per sales dollar
Increase dealer outlets by $x\%$
Increase sales force by $x\%$
Open $x$ number of new territories

Personnel

Reduce absenteeism by $x\%$
Reduce labor turnover by $x\%$
Reduce complaints by $x\%$
Increase number of written suggestions by $x\%$
Double the number of formal training hours
Double the number of job applicants
Double the number of employees given first aid training
Explain insurance program annually
Appraise performance of all employees annually
Ensure that appraisal interviews are held
Introduce annual physical examination for all supervisors
Post all job vacancies
Initiate executive development

Profitability

Increase net profit dollars by $x\%$
Increase profit per sales dollar by $x\%$
Increase profit as percentage of assets by $x\%$
Increase gross profit margin by $x\%$
Increase current asset ratio by $x\%$
Reduce taxes by $x\%$
Reduce G&A expense by $x\%$
Reduce accounts receivable by $x\%$

Management

Undertake long-range planning
Install new system of controls
Improve interdepartmental cooperation
Change capital structure
Broaden scope of research
Decentralize the organization
Install electronic computer

Applying MBO to staff functions raises different problems than applying MBO to line. Typical staff functions are personnel, public relations, engineering, research, controller, and office management. Here the goals are mostly qualitative. Results are evaluated by judgment rather than by measurement. These limitations should not, however, prevent a company from applying MBO to staff departments. If a specific goal can be phrased in understandable words, a standard already exists. So results can be judged and rewards and recognition for accomplishment are possible.

**MBO as a Specific Problem Solver**

MBO can be highly effective as a specific problem solver. One of the greatest difficulties with cost reduction efforts, for example, is that blanket cost-cutting goals are imposed by top management on the entire organization, regardless of whether the overall target is appropriate or even feasible for some functions.

Bell Helicopter Company attacked this problem with success by using an MBO type of approach to reduce costs. Although the company calls its approach a "cost awareness program" (CAP), it is not a single program, but many. The CAP manager does not set cost-reduction objectives, but meets with the manager of each function to negotiate objectives. The function manager has the specific knowledge needed to identify activities where cost reduction is possible, to set objectives and money figures, and to devise a plan of action. Therefore he also manages the cost-reduction program he has planned, with the help of his own subordinate managers plus information and assistance from the CAP staff.

CAP uses several approaches characteristic of a successful MBO cost-reduction program. Most importantly, mutual goal setting is emphasized. The overall corporate goal of reducing costs is initiated by top management, which has the best knowledge of overall needs. The more limited goals and the means of achieving them are set by the people who must actually do the achieving. By participating in setting the goals, they develop the strength of commitment that is essential.

Information about cost-reduction goals flows freely between management levels. The CAP staff provides information about cost-reduction needs to the managers of the various functions. It also gathers information on progress from the different functions and passes it on to higher management.

Obviously, the goal-setting process is crucial to the success of management by objectives. Where can it go wrong? The most common problems fall into four broad categories: (1) Goals themselves are inappropriate. (2) The method of measuring progress toward the goals is inappropriate. (3) Management's attitudes are inadequate. (4) Responsibilities are not clearly and appropriately fixed. Sometimes managers have not been involved at all stages of the development of an MBO program. When standards are lacking or unattainable, MBO will fail.

Successful management by objectives forces managers to delegate. Without the delegation of authority and responsibility, the established objectives can't be achieved. MBO is a system of strict accountability and one which calls for participation at all levels. It is a way of management with a future.

## REVIEW

Compare "decentralization" and "delegation."

Name the three principal elements in the "circle of delegation."

Analyze your own job in the format of Figure 17.

Name at least six specific authorities which might be delegated.

Define the exception principle.

How should an MBO program unfold?

Name three *objectives* in production and three in marketing.

# 12

# HOW TO MANAGE INNOVATION

Without innovation, people would still be living in caves. Innovation means the introduction of something new—a new idea, method, or device. Managing innovation calls for planning, organizing, controlling, and coordinating the creation or introduction of something new.

Innovation is more than just modification of the way things are done. Admittedly it's hard to draw the line between a change and an innovation. The latter introduces some completely new element. Risk is greater than with change. The future determines whether an innovation was sensible, while the effects of change are usually calculable.

Innovation ability is creative, conceptual, and rare. It can, however, be fed in an encouraging environment or stifled by mismanagement. Some managers would rather let well enough alone. To do so makes life easier. Some people talk about returning to the good old days even though they never lived through them.

Other people fear for the environment if innovation is not managed with environmental safeguards. There have been many books written and speeches given that management's greatest task in the future will be meeting the challenge of change. Actually, its greatest challenge now is managing innovation.

## Innovative Procedures

Changing an office system from single to double entry bookkeeping can scarcely be termed innovation. However, change from handwritten records to computerization is considered an innovative change of procedure. Since radical changes involve altering work habits, they encounter considerable employee resistance. Also they make training in the new ways necessary. To the extent that employees have been involved in setting up new procedures, acceptance is easier to get. Smart managers assign key employees to finding and setting up new procedures.

Time and motion study was an innovation 50 years ago. Now it is an accepted management technique. Scores of historical innovations have followed the same route. Most managerial innovations are aimed at increasing production, improving quality, or lowering costs.

Usually an innovative procedure is devised to overcome a specific problem, such as a production bottleneck. Tackling problems as they crop up is less effective than an organized, continuing, widescale attack on working, managerial, and production methods. Developing innovative procedures should be a continuing process.

## Innovative Equipment

Innovative procedures are usually generated internally. Innovative equipment usually comes from outside suppliers. Since competing suppliers claim their products are best, selecting new equipment that's just right is difficult.

Here is a simple plan to help make a proper decision on selecting new equipment. Make a list of all claims for and features of equipment under consideration. Include cost, output, tolerances, space required, setup time, other uses, estimated maintenance costs, probable useful life, and training requirements.

If three manufacturers are in the running, allot three columns on the same sheet with the names of the manufacturers as headings.

Use a simple rating code such as the following: N—necessary, U—unnecessary, H—helpful. Apply these code letters in each column to each feature listed. This analytic rating sheet will usually show which piece of equipment should be purchased.

## Innovative Policies

In the glossary of terms in Chapter 1, a policy was defined as "a standing decision for a recurring problem, subject to change as conditions demand." This definition provides for policy innovation. Here are same examples:

- ☐ A company that has consistently fought unions suddenly decides to work cooperatively with them.
- ☐ A firm allows executives to take temporary positions in the federal government on a loan basis.
- ☐ Instead of working through wholesalers, a company decides to set up its own retail outlets.

All three of these would be such radical changes of policy as to be classed as innovative. When new management comes into a company, it usually puts innovative policies into effect.

- ☐ Public relations supplies another example of innovative policies. Modern managers believe that their organizations are part of the community. Employees are encouraged to participate in community activities, get involved in local politics, community fund raising, and other projects. Innovative public relations makes companies good neighbors.
- ☐ Many companies are adopting another innovative policy. They participate in social change, urban redevelopment, aid to minority businesses, improvement of the environment, support of ethical practices, and betterment of education and family life. These companies have come a long way from the earlier managerial practice of refraining from involvement.

## Product Innovation

Many companies have unprofitable products in their line but hesitate to eliminate them for fear of reducing sales volume. Ideally, companies find new products to push out the old.

There are other reasons besides cutting losses for developing new products and services. Buyer preferences change. People prefer automatic shift in cars to manual shift, though in sports cars manual shifts are back in favor. Long-range planning means examining the gap between where a company is now and where it wants to be in five years. This highlights needs for product innovation. Competition forces innovation.

New needs arise from technological change. For example, an electronic company foresees that greater use of computers will increase the demand for component parts.

Market research and questions raised by customers call for product innovation. There are four principal ways to add new products:

1. Imitate products sold by competitors.
2. Acquire companies which already make different products.
3. Through market research, identify specific customer needs and create products to meet them.
4. Develop new products through company research.

The first two are fairly obvious, although they may cause special problems of patents, royalties, production, marketing, credit, and the like.

Marketing research may identify a customer need or pinpoint a particularly profitable product. Normally, research will also uncover ideas on distribution, warehousing, pricing, packaging, and sales promotion. Marketing research is a better initial way to develop new products than is laboratory research.

Many companies waste technical research by failing to direct it. Only giant corporations can afford pure or fundamental research. Most companies have to put their scientists to work on applied research seeking new products, equipment, or methods. It's management's responsibility to coordinate all parts of the business. By neglecting to direct, coordinate, and control research and development personnel, management leaves them without overview leadership.

R&D thinking should be oriented to organization objectives. Key people in research and development need to understand management goals, company strengths and weaknesses, and the economics of survival. Research money can't be spent on interesting projects which offer little hope of profit.

Most companies have so many proposals for new products and services that they must use some screening method to find the best ones. Frequently, a committee is formed for this purpose. The committee lists the factors to judge profitability of a proposal. Separately, the committee members rate each proposal and bring their findings together for discussion. This method screens out most suggestions.

The remaining ones are discussed further or referred to the R&D department for technical feasibility. The R&D department should submit its recommendations but should not be allowed to make the final decision or to undertake additional research without approval.

Any company studying new products can profit by this checklist of things to consider when developing new products:

**Why?**

1. *For sales volume:*
   To offset declines in some products.
   To add to sales volume.
   To increase percentage share of market.
   To diversify against consumer demand changes.
2. *For cost reasons:*
   To keep production facilities busy.
   To regularize peaks and valleys in production.
   To spread selling expenses over a broader sales volume.
3. *For competitive reasons:*
   To match competitor's products.
   To make product line more complete.
   To strive for industry leadership.
   To establish a prestige product.
4. *For greater utilization of company resources:*
   To use available capital.
   To benefit from established distribution channels.
   To get greater productivity from available manpower.
   To use specialized knowledge of key employees.
   To use present by-products.

**What Is the Market?**

1. *Who would be the users?*
   Is their need now being met, or must demand be created?
   What are their attitudes and buying habits?
   What is the total present and potential dollar volume?
   What share of this market can be expected now and in the future?
2. *What competition exists?*
   Same or similar products: price, sales volume, acceptance, profitability.
   Superiority of proposed product: quality, price, service, use, availability.
3. *What is the selling problem?*
   Advertising and promotion.

Sell through present, or a new, sales force?
Training sales force.
Transportation, warehousing, and servicing.
Influence of economic trends.

**How to Affect Production**

1. *Capital expenditures:*
   For research and development.
   For tools and equipment.
   For manufacturing, shipping, storage space.
   Length of capital payout period.
2. *Procurement:*
   Raw materials: sources, specifications, prices.
   Storage and handling.
3. *Estimated costs:*
   Material.
   Labor: direct and indirect.
   Manufacturing overhead allocation.
4. *Personnel:*
   How many new employees?
   Selection and training.
   Supervision needed.

**Producing a New Product**

1. Prepare product specifications.
2. Produce small quantity in laboratory, shop, or pilot plant.
3. Test product under difficult conditions.
4. Test product against consumer acceptance and use.
5. Modify specifications, production methods.

**Marketing the New Product**

1. Select test markets.
2. Prepare a budget.
3. Set up a cost accounting plan.
4. Analyze experience in test markets.
5. Extend selling program to entire market.
6. Lay out a three- to five-year plan for the new product.
7. Annually, check execution of the plan.

The introduction of a new product brings up many new problems. Specialists must be employed for researching, designing, producing, and marketing the new product. New capital equipment must be purchased; inventory levels, manufacturing, and storage space must be determined. Studies are needed for new working methods, new skills for operatives, and new materials.

Advertising and sales promotion campaigns have to be created. Decisions must be made on credit policies, warehousing, and physical distribution. New products bring up legal questions such as patents, contracts, and sales agreements.

Few new products survive even one year. The selection of new products is a risky and complicated matter. Yet every company must put some resources into new product development to survive. Product life cycles are too unpredictable to neglect this aspect of every business.

## Managing the Innovators

Business decisions depend more and more on mathematics, science, and specialized technologies. Many problems which land on the top executive's desk involve important technical decisions. Yet by education and experience he may be poorly equipped to make them. So he must combine pieces of information into a whole by relying on competent advice from his technical staff.

However, industrial managers have not always been successful in supervising high-grade technical people, who are usually more interested in ideas, mathematics, and mechanics than in human relations. Managers, on the other hand, spend more time on people questions. Organization methods which simplify managers' jobs may complicate those of professionals. The professional is often considered temperamental. He may secretly believe that his intellect and training make him superior to his nontechnical manager. Yet the ability to manage people, to get things done through them, is a rarer talent than technical knowledge. If the professional is the brains of an organization, then the manager is its heart.

Industry therefore is faced with the choice of putting pressures on scientists and other professionals to conform to the organization or allowing them to pursue their goals as they see fit. Successful managers meet this dilemma by delegating those parts of management for which technical men are best equipped, such as planning technical programs, establishing standards, and setting up project controls.

Top managers can use budgeting and progress reports to retain control over the innovators. Research results flow through the managers to other departments. In this way, while scientists are allowed latitude of action, higher-level managers retain final control.

Some companies carry out this concept by assigning an administrative assistant to each technical group. He serves as a communication bridge between scientists and executive control. He maintains the budget, prepares progress reports, informs management, and prepares abstracts and summaries of research projects. In most cases he is an administrator with an educational background similar to the scientists in the department.

Compensating technical men has created some problems. Working up the managerial ladder is the usual route to top salaries. Yet many technical people have no desire to follow that route. Indeed, it often isn't in their best interests or the company's to turn technical people into managers. Some companies, General Electric for one, have answered this vital compensation question by establishing an "independent contributor" category with its own grade and pay scales apart from the management group's.

## Creativity

Innovation implies creativity. Someone, somewhere has had an "idea whose time has come." Managers have no monopoly on creativity, as companies with well-run suggestion systems know. Mavericks sometimes prove to be the most creative. Some large companies have developed creativity training programs, but any manager can increase creativity in himself and in his subordinates. Man is an ingenious animal—especially so when faced with challenge. Creative imagination is a natural aptitude, but one that gets little exercise.

The management of innovation has to include encouragement of creativity. A simple way to encourage creativity begins with setting a specific objective: an obstacle to be overcome, a problem to be solved, an object to be made, a course of action to be followed. Then, collecting relevant information takes place. Imagination starts where existing knowledge leaves off. All ideas are solicited, no matter how impractical or far-out. Creativity seldom strikes like a bolt from the blue. More often, it springs from the perseverence of knowledgeable persons.

Creative persons often clash with the establishment. They may challenge the status quo and advance way-out ideas. Unfortunately, many unimaginative, maladjusted individuals show similiar traits. Sometimes it's hard to differentiate imagination from radicalism. The keys to handling creative employees are challenge, facilities, opportunity, freedom of action, encouragement, and recognition.

Brainstorming is a means of developing group creativity. It has a few accepted rules:

Unusual, or even impractical, ideas are welcomed.
No criticism of any idea is allowed.
Many ideas are solicited.
Combinations of ideas are encouraged.
"Selling" of any idea is discouraged.
Ideas are evaluated by the group.

The brainstorming method became almost a fad some years ago, and as a result, it fell into disfavor in many companies. Yet its method is fundamentally sound. It has a place in managing innovation.

## REVIEW

What is your definition of innovation?

Name four areas of business where innovation can be useful.

How would you compare the merits of three competitive desk calculators?

Give two examples of policy change toward social problems.

Name four ways a company can add to its line of products.

What is brainstorming and how does it work?

# 13

# MANAGEMENT POLICIES AND LABOR RELATIONS

The word "policy" is used to mean many different things. Here are three examples which illustrate different uses:

- ☐ It is the policy of this company to provide high-quality goods and services to our customers.
- ☐ Management policy permits a dealer to return unsold goods within six months of date of purchase.
- ☐ Because of fire hazard, no smoking is permitted in the plant.

Although these examples are loosely called "management policy," the first one is a *management philosophy*, the second a *policy*, and the third a *rule*. There is no agreement among authorities in management on the distinctions among the three terms. In fact they are frequently used interchangeably. Some writers tell what each term is supposed to do rather than attempting to define it. In this chapter we shall try to distinguish among them.

## Management Philosophy

Management philosophy is a system of beliefs to guide an organization on objectives, standards of performance, and relationships with society. Under this definition a *philosophy of management* is a group of related ideas, a body of knowledge, a series of integrated attitudes. It must be brought down to earth through a number of guiding *policies,* and these in turn must be made specific through *rules.* Both policies and rules must be consistent with the basic management philosophy.

Most statements of company policy contain a mixture of philosophy and policy. A few contain rules.

Many top executives find it a challenging job to write out company philosophy. It is related to that hazy term "company image." It provides the backdrop against which the corporate activities are acted out.

A philosophy is positive rather than negative. It rarely restrains action. Although designed to last for a long time, it is not unchangeable. As times change, it may be necessary to change philosophy, policies, and rules. Change in any one of these three will eventually affect the other two. When they are not consistent with one another, much conflict can arise. So it's important when changing one to consider whether modifications need to be made in either of the other two. To avoid confusion, management philosophy, policies, and rules need to be spelled out clearly in writing.

## Policies

A definition of policy is, "A statement of guidelines for decisions and prescribed courses of action for handling problems." For example, a narrow policy might state, "This company will pay average or better wage rates for employees in our community." A broader policy might state, "Management will annually review wage rates, taking into account community wage levels, changes in the cost of living, and profitability of the company."

Policies are not inviolate. For example, at one time a company had a policy that if an employee punched in his time card one or more minutes late he would be docked a half-hour's pay. Employees resented this policy. They would sit idle until the half-hour had expired. Finally, agreements with an employees' committee came up with a two-part policy:

1. Employees not on assembly line jobs could make up the time lost by lateness after regular working hours.

2. Those on assembly lines would lose pay only for the actual time lost. To get the line moving on time, management could substitute another employee.

The new policy did not cure lateness, but it did improve morale.

Recently with the lessening of authoritarian management, policies have become more flexible. Discretionary limits may be set for those to be guided by a policy. Usually any limits written into a policy are designed to stop a too liberal interpretation in one department as against a very strict interpretation in another—a situation that leads to conflict.

Policies reduce the need for close supervision by higher-level managers. At the same time they offer greater freedom of thought and action by lower-level managers. They increase possibilities for pushing decisions down to lower levels. This helps develop more managers to apply policy within their areas of responsibility.

Sometimes policies are set by a small group of top executives. The modern approach brings into the writing of any policy those affected by it. Such participation prevents some misunderstandings, resistance, loopholes, or other ambiguities. Frequently, it uncovers the need for broader policies.

Policies are not easy to express in writing. Word usage enters. For example, does the word "equitable" mean the same thing to the person who wrote it as to the person who reads it?

Some policies apply to the company as a whole and must be consistent with management philosophy. Other policies apply to certain functions of the business, such as production or sales. For example, in one company, salesmen were reimbursed for all travel expense while service personnel had to work with a fixed daily expense allowance. To avoid inconsistencies like this, periodic reviews of all written policies of all departments should be made.

Within different departments, policies are implemented by specific directives and rules. An example would be the exact procedures for submitting an expense account for approval.

Often, tradition has become policy without anyone questioning whether it is applicable to current conditions. Usually, a tradition hasn't been reduced to writing. When an attempt is made to do so, it's sometimes found to be very poor policy. In one large insurance company it was traditional for the assistant to be promoted to the department head's position when it was vacated. No one had questioned this tradition until a capable young man became available. It was obvious to top management that the less able assistant should definitely *not* be the one promoted. Policies are useless without rules, directives, and procedures to carry them out.

Since laws change, policies can conflict with new state or federal legislation. Governmental agencies establish mandatory standards, and past company policy may conflict with newly issued regulations. OSHA (Occupational Safety and Health Act) has had a tremendous impact on industry practices in the 1970s. Policies in employee relations, including union relations, are more subject to change than in any other area.

Companies may set up policy manuals for different levels of the organization. There may be one for office workers, plant workers, supervisors, and higher management and even one for confidential use of the board of directors.

## Rules

Policies are subject to interpretation; rules are not. A rule is a statement of a specific action to be followed or to be avoided under certain conditions. Employee rule books usually spell out the do's and don'ts as well as give information on insurance, paydays, hours of work, vacations, and so on.

Rules allow little latitude for discretion. They say, "Do this" or "Don't do that." Management that depends entirely on a system of rules is so rigid that it will cause many employee relations problems. On the other hand, rules do help to locate trouble when production or quality is not being met. Somewhere a rule or a standard has been violated. Also, it is easier for employees, when guided by the rules, to understand and follow them.

Rules can be useful when applicable to the organization as a whole. One bad effect, though, is that rules may cause bypassing of middle managers. Since they leave little discretion, they tend to reduce middle managers' self-image. They see themselves as robots carrying out orders from on high.

It is unjust for some departments to enforce a certain rule and others not. When this situation occurs, it should be corrected quickly. Sometimes rules can result in supervisors' failing to act on justifiable exceptions, or passing the buck to higher managers. Highly complex rules can cause delays or confusion or both.

Employee and supervisors who consciously evade rules tend to feel guilty. They try to keep the evasion from their superiors even though they feel it is justified. The disadvantages of rules only point up to the fact that they must be very carefully drawn. If they are, rules can be a useful management tool.

## Industrial Relations Policies

Many policies, and most rules, apply to relationships with employees: hiring, training, compensation, and supervision. Additional policies and rules pertain to benefits such as life insurance, medical insurance, retirement, vacations, holidays. Others apply to overtime, sickness, absenteeism, lateness, smoking, fighting, loafing, and the like.

Labor shortages and changing employee attitudes have caused many managements to reduce the number of rules and to offer greater latitude in application of policies. Modern management allows greater freedom of action to employees, permitting them to make many job decisions. Top management has greater awareness that workers are human beings with intellects and emotions. Public opinion, union and legislative pressures, and enlightened managers have contributed to this change in viewpoint. It has also been influenced by the findings of social scientists.

## Relations with Unions

Management policies toward unions provide an acid test of wisdom. The history of unionism is one of rising power consciousness coupled with rising expectations. This is true in most of the economically advanced countries.

Approximately 30 percent of American workers belong to organized unions. Their bargaining power has brought higher wages to their members. Higher earnings, when not accompanied by productivity increases, have contributed to the inflationary spiral.

Management attitudes have generally been antagonistic to unionism. Fifty years ago unionism was violently opposed: Management did everything in its power to keep unions from being formed. When a strike was called, companies attempted lockouts and strikebreakers were hired. Full-scale battles were waged between strikers and hired private police.

In the intervening years the power of unions has steadily increased, partly due to support by federal and state legislation. In recent years, most companies have softened their stand against the union movement. A succession of labor laws has restrained management's freedom of action but has also put restraints on union abuse of power.

Serious students of management will conclude that in this century managers have failed to take the initiative in fulfilling obligations to society, as people in general and workers in particular interpret those obligations. So credit for most social legislation is given legislators and labor leaders. There is some evidence that the current generation of managers will not be equally shortsighted.

An example of legislative pressure is the minimum wage. Increases in the minimum wage force changes in the entire wage structure with far-reaching effects on wage and salary administration. It has become a vote-getting device for politicians, a preventive of labor exploitation, and a method of enforced sharing of wealth. For several decades the minimum rate has increased faster than average wage rates, the cost of living, or the gross national product. Here are some pros and cons on the minimum wage:

| For | Against |
|---|---|
| Increases purchasing power of lower-paid employees. | Increases labor costs, prices, and inflation. |
| Reduces burden on government relief agencies. | Increases unemployment of teenagers and marginal workers. |
| Forces training of unskilled workers. | Compresses pay differential between unskilled and skilled workers. |
| May reduce discontent of marginal workers. | Contributes to labor turnover and absenteeism. |
| Builds self-esteem because of earnings instead of charity. | May bankrupt marginally profitable firms. |
| Promotes greater use of efficient mechanization. | |

**Strikes**

The strike has been organized labor's most potent weapon. In prolonged strikes the taxpayer, who may be seriously inconvenienced or financially hurt, actually subsidizes the unions. Government and other public funds support strikers. Welfare payments and mortgage payment support are examples.

However, the rising affluence of some union members makes them less inclined to strike. When they were earning 50 or 60 cents an hour, they had little to lose by striking. Wages are so high today that in a long strike workers have little chance of getting an increase large enough to offset the loss of income. Moreover, many workers have moved to the suburbs, have comfortable homes, have one or two cars, and are putting their children through college. Their expenses are so high that they could not go for any long period of time on the strike benefits plus any welfare benefits they can get. In income and status they've joined the middle class.

### Unionism Is Changing

Some union leaders privately admit that the strike may be obsolete. They are more willing to accept binding arbitration. At one time, labor demands were concentrated on wages, hours, and working conditions. Currently they are likely to cover:

- Reasonable wage increases.
- Cost-of-living clauses.
- Profit sharing.
- Improvements in insurance and retirement benefits.
- Short-term contracts with renegotiation clauses.
- The right to refuse overtime.
- A voice in work going to outside contractors, in major technological changes, in contemplated plant closing, or in layoffs.

White collar workers—office, engineering and technical—have seen the success of unions. They have suffered buying power erosion from inflation and job insecurity caused by technological change. As a consequence, they have become more susceptible to union organizing efforts. Foremen and supervisors, resenting lack of authority and nonparticipation in decisions affecting them, are turning an interested ear to organizing efforts. Top managers are conscious of the white collar movement. Many are taking constructive steps to offset it by becoming more responsive to social, environmental, and ecological questions.

Unions in industries where wage levels are still low see the strike as a useful weapon, and they feel confident that welfare and strike benefits will be sufficient to see a union through a prolonged strike if necessary.

With the backing of federal laws and standards, future shop stewards and union committeemen are likely to become more important, at least in improving working conditions. Some companies welcome the efforts of these union representatives to avert or settle complaints, or to point out the failures of foremen. Where union representatives cooperate with foremen, their efforts become an extension of supervision.

With growing acceptance of unionism by employers, accompanied by greater social responsibility by labor leaders, a give-and-take has come about between unions and employers, which is a good sign for the future.

Part of this new attitude stems from the realization by many union leaders that their members are competing with workers in foreign countries. They realize it is necessary to cooperate with employers to step up productivity. Many employers have felt the effects of foreign competition for a long time, but only recently have union leaders and members left their long-standing free trade position.

Employees are coming to realize that seniority rules, limitations of production, duplication of effort, featherbedding, inflexibility in work assignments, jurisdictional disputes among crafts, and various union-created work rules are harmful to their own welfare. It is reasonable to expect that the years ahead will show greater cooperation between employers and unions for the benefit of both parties and society in general.

Management by objectives is a strong force in current management practice. It began with line managers but is spreading to staff specialists as well. The future should see the concepts of MBO carried to negotiations with unions. Companies have engaged in "productivity bargaining" whereby added employee benefits are bargained for changes of work practice, for increased production, or to meet agreed upon objectives. This approach hints of joint cooperation or a management-objectives concept between unions and management.

## REVIEW

Compare the terms "management philosophy," "policy," and "rule."

Why, in recent years, have policies become more flexible?

What are some risks for a company that has too many rules?

Why is the collective bargaining power of unions strong?

Name some pros and cons of setting minimum wages by law.

Why are union members becoming less inclined to strike?

# 14

# GETTING RESULTS FROM OUTSIDE EXPERTS

More than half a century ago Harrington Emerson, a well-known management engineer and contemporary of Frederick W. Taylor, wrote a book entitled *The Twelve Principles of Efficiency*. One of the 12 principles was "Get competent counsel." The advice is still good today, because no manager can be an expert on all subjects.

Businessmen have long since learned that if they have legal problems they should consult a lawyer; construction problems, a construction engineer; auditing problems, an outside auditor. This practice has sometimes been forced on business managers by law or administrative rulings. However, for other problems, many businessmen feel that they can find solutions by themselves. In many cases businessmen make decisions based on inadequate knowledge or experience. Eventually they pay for their mistakes.

In general, it's cheaper and more efficient to call in an outside consultant for a one-time project. Examples are a new filing system, a job evaluation, production scheduling, a management audit, a computer feasibility study, or a decision on a plant site location.

When employing a consultant, follow this checklist:

1. Contact former clients to learn their opinions.

2. Have a staff man assigned who has the kind of experience needed to offer advice.

3. Get detailed recommendations on how to solve problems, not just what should be done. Retain the consultant's services until the recommended program is operating successfully.

4. Assign to work with the consultant's staff representative *two* associates who will become familiar with any new program.

5. Put financial understandings in writing. Consulting fees are increasing rapidly. Get firm bids on total costs.

## Legal Assistance

The majority of small and medium-size companies cannot afford a full-time lawyer on the payroll, so they must depend on calling in a law firm or a local lawyer as legal problems arise. However, even large firms with legal departments often retain outside counsel. Since lawyers specialize and laws have become so complex, lawyers with expertise must be found to handle the special legal problems which come up.

Many companies find it wise to elect an attorney to the board of directors. He should be well versed in corporation law, antitrust legislation, federal contracts, public liability, insurance, taxes, or other areas of particular concern. In a recent three-year period the number of lawsuits filed against companies in federal district courts jumped from 6,743 to 10,479!

An employer can subscribe to published services which will often give him current information on problems in particular areas. An excellent example of such an area is labor law and its interpretation. A competent personnel manager will acquaint himself with all laws pertaining to his job and keep abreast of changes and interpretations. In this way he may be able to keep his company out of problems that otherwise would require legal advice or court action. But, he should be careful not to try to substitute his judgment for legal advice. He is not qualified to practice law.

Here is some of the significant federal legislation with which managers should be familiar:

- ☐ The National Labor Relations Act of 1935, which encouraged the formation of unions and collective bargaining and defined unfair labor practices.

- ☐ The Taft-Hartley Act of 1947, which sought to establish a better balance between employers and unions and to remove Communists from positions of power in unions. The Act also required unions to file financial statements and aimed to make them more responsible financially and socially.
- ☐ The Landrum-Griffin Act of 1959, which required employers and unions to file reports and disclose information on salaries, trust funds, insurance, and the like.
- ☐ The Federal Fair Labor Standards Act of 1938 (wage and hour law).
- ☐ The Civil Rights Law of 1965, which aimed at preventing discrimination in employment and employment practices.
- ☐ The Equal Rights for Women Act of 1963 (amendment to the Fair Labor Standards Act).
- ☐ The Equal Employment Opportunity Act of 1964.
- ☐ The Occupational Safety and Health Act of 1970.

In addition, there are many state laws on compensation for industrial accidents, wages and hours, and some of the other areas covered by the above listing.

Most of the features of these laws and the interpretive rulings which have followed can be understood by an intelligent personnel manager. They are cited as examples of internal information which should be available to help keep a company out of some legal entanglements.

In other fields there are equally good sources of information on taxes, insurance, traffic, auditing, sales contracts, and the like. Many publishers issue reports for managers which cover special topics and up-to-date developments.

## MANAGEMENT CONSULTANTS

According to the Association of Consulting Management Engineers (ACME), there are approximately 2,600 management consulting firms in the United States and Canada. They range in size from one-man firms to those with hundreds of people on the professional staff. The smaller firms usually specialize in one or two areas of business, such as finance or marketing. Or they may specialize by kind of industry. The larger firms offer clients a wide range of services to many kinds of organizations. Management consultants offer the following services:

- ☐ A comprehensive management audit: organization structure; mergers; ecology.
- ☐ Organization planning: long-range planning: management information system; computers; controls; decentralization; decision making.
- ☐ Production management: purchasing; production control; inventory; industrial engineering; costs; plant maintenance and equipment; critical path planning.
- ☐ Marketing: surveys; advertising; product innovation; sales force; policies; pricing.
- ☐ Personnel: policies; selection; training; compensation; manpower development; communication; motivation.

Competent management consultants bring a fresh, objective viewpoint to many problems. They provide specialized knowledge and experience and relieve busy managers of the need to tackle complex or one-time situations. Using consultants avoids the expense of adding specialists to the payroll.

The Association of Consulting Management Engineers offers these guidelines for getting the best use from management consultants:

1. Consultants should be selected with extreme care. Former clients should be contacted to determine if the consultant can meet the client's requirements.

2. The project must be clearly defined in both the client's and the consultant's minds. This is usually set down in a proposal letter. Agreement must be reached with the consultant on the obligations of each party, including fees. As mentioned previously, the consultant's work must be supervised through periodic meetings.

3. The company must require its own personnel to furnish reports on carrying out the consultant's recommendations.

## PERSONNEL CONSULTANTS

Because of its growing importance, many specialized consulting firms offer counsel on all aspects of employee relations, including labor law. Their services cover selection, training, communication, compensation, health, fringe benefits, safety, working conditions, recordkeeping, collective bargaining, arbitration, pensions, and insurance.

Some personnel management advice can be obtained without charge from insurance carriers and from government agencies.

## Accounting

Most companies need far more complicated accounting systems than single- or double-entry bookkeeping. Income tax reporting and the desirability of an internal cost-finding system require them. Internal auditing to prevent errors and fraud becomes important as companies grow.

The accounting procedures of a company generally grow haphazardly. Accounts receivable become more numerous so a bookkeeping machine is purchased. The company buys different machines for check preparation and payroll. Accounts payable may be recorded manually. A flip card file keeps track of inventory. Eventually a computer salesman persuades management that electronic data processing can take over all accounting activities.

Corporations with many outside stockholders have their annual statements audited and certified by independent certified public accountants. Outside accountants are often used to prepare company tax returns. They can give advice on internal controls over inventory, safeguards on cash receipts and disbursements, handling payrolls, and many other operations in both plant and office. Because these experts encounter these same matters on other assignments, companies can benefit from cross-fertilization of ideas and methods.

Managers should not ask outside accountants for advice on management. Most reputable public accountants wisely and rightly are not inclined to give management advice. Some of the largest public accounting firms, however, do have separate management consulting divisions. They can be retained for a fee to perform many of the same kinds of consulting jobs as are done by management consultants. Many small, new businesses retain a public accountant to handle all bookkeeping and accounting functions.

## Finance

A bank can be more than a repository of funds or a source of loans. Most banks offer many services which are valuable to businesses. Top managers of successful companies always have close relationships with bank officers. Bank officers know a lot about businessmen and businesses in the community—their integrity, credit rating, and often their plans. While bankers must be circumspect in dealing with their customers, they are a source of influence and information of great value.

Commercial bankers are not directly concerned with raising capital, lending for a term of more than five years (unless there are fixed assets of a real property nature involved), or advising on capital investment. Raising permanent capital, or equity, brings in the investment banker.

Investment bankers and financial consultants are needed for the sale of stock by new or established corporations or the issuance of bonds. Scores of steps are required to meet regulations of the Securities and Exchange Commission, underwriters, and the National Association of Securities Dealers, as well as state securities laws, and therefore experienced investment and legal talent is required.

Investment bankers may arrange private financing for long-term capital rather than underwriting a public issue of stock. Their fund sources are pension funds, wealthy individuals, foundations, insurance companies, or venture capitalists. Such suppliers of capital usually place restrictions on its use and on company management.

## Industrial Engineering

Industrial engineering consulting applies principally to production. Its scope normally includes layout, flow of work, materials handling, equipment, production planning, costing, inventory control, time study, motion study, incentive pay systems, operations research, and quality control.

Sometimes free counsel is available from manufacturers of machinery, materials-handling equipment, trucking companies, heating and ventilating engineers, and electric utilities. "Free counsel" is not really an accurate term since the company giving advice expects to get back its investment by selling equipment, goods, or services.

Many industrial engineering consultants are only concerned with time and motion economy. Too few consultants consider total systems concepts, mathematical models, and computer-controlled production. So basic needs should be analyzed before hiring a consultant in this field.

Many large advertising agencies have developed into marketing counselors. As such, they can advise on advertising copy and media, sales promotion, radio and television, market research, selection and training of salesmen, selling methods, control of salesmen and sales expenses, new products, contracts, franchises, distribution channels, and applicable legislation.

The close contact and personal interest of the owner of a small advertising agency may well offset the impersonality of a large agency.

In addition there are consultants who specialize in many marketing areas, listed above, but do not prepare advertising copy for use in publications.

Direct mail is one such, especially for "rifle-shot" selling to a selective list of prospects. Rising postal rates are making "scatter-shot" direct mail too costly for most products.

Consumer research in particular needs expertise in training interviewers, preparing questionnaires, selecting representative sampling, doing adequate statistical analyses, and drawing proper conclusions. Whereas market research may depend largely on available statistics, consumer research gathers data from potential customers.

## Sources of Information

There are many sources of information, statistical data, or technical advice. Libraries have cross-reference books such as *A Brief Guide to Sources of Scientific and Technical Information; Business Information—How to Find and Use It; Research Centers Directory; Business Periodical Index;* and *Applied Science and Technology Index.*

### The Department of Commerce

Publications and services of the Department of Commerce can be of great assistance to any business. Their scope is indicated by the following subdivisions of the department:

1. *Bureau of the Census*, which publishes:
   - ☐ *The Census of Business: Retail Trade, Wholesale Trade, Selected Services, Public Warehousing.*
   - ☐ *The Census of Manufactures: Mineral Industries, Annual Surveys of Manufactures, Standard Industrial Classifica-*

*tion Manual, County Business Patterns, Manufacturing Employees* (payrolls, production, value of shipments, value added by manufacture, inventories, and reports by industry, area, subject, etc.), and the *Statistical Abstract of the United States*.

2. Office of Business Economics, which publishes the *Survey of Current Business* and other economic data.
3. Bureau of Domestic Commerce, which has field offices in the principal cities of the United States for dissemination of business information.
4. Bureau of International Commerce, which provides services and information regarding foreign countries.
5. Other bureaus and offices of the Department of Commerce include the Economic Development Administration, the Patent Office, the National Technical Information Service, the Office of Minority Business Enterprise, the Maritime Administration, and the National Bureau of Standards.

Reorganization and transfer of government bureaus occur from time to time and new services are added.

**Other Sources**

Government departments other than the Department of Commerce that are sources of business information include the departments of Labor; Agriculture; the Interior; Transportation; and Health, Education and Welfare; as well as the Internal Revenue Service. Other sources include:

*Federal Reserve Bulletin*
Dun & Bradstreet
Federal Trade Commission
Securities and Exchange Commission
*The Fortune Directory* of largest companies
*Sales Management* (survey of buying power)
Thomas Register of American Manufacturers
*Moody's Industrial Manual*
*Standard & Poor's Register*
Better Business Bureaus
Chambers of commerce
Various books and magazines

The many societies and associations devoted to various aspects of business or technology also provide useful information. Some are listed below. Most of them publish a periodical of some sort and have a headquarters office. The address can be obtained from a good library.

Administrative Management Society
Air Freight Forwarders Association
American Academy of Occupational Medicine
American Accounting Association
American Advertising Federation
American Arbitration Association
American Bar Association
American Chemical Society
American Federation of Information Processing Societies
American Industrial Hygiene Association
American Institute of Industrial Engineers
American Management Associations
American Marketing Association
American Materials Handling Society
American Records Management Association
American Society of Mechanical Engineers
American Society of Personnel Administration
American Society for Quality Control
American Society of Safety Engineers
American Society of Traffic and Transportation
American Society for Training and Development
Association for Systems Management
Chamber of Commerce of the United States
The Conference Board
Council of Profit Sharing Industries
Credit Union National Association
Data Processing Management Association
Financial Executives Institute
Industrial Management Society
International Association of Business Communicators
National Association of Credit Management
National Association of Manufacturers
National Association of Purchasing Management
National Safety Council
Occupational Health Institute
Operations Research Society of America
Packaging Institute
Public Relations Society of America
Sales and Marketing Executives International
Society for Personnel Administration
Associated Traffic Clubs

Managers must learn to integrate the knowledge and efforts of varied specialists: engineers, mathematicians, accountants, lawyers, economists, sociologists, computer programmers, market researchers, salespeople. They must be able to communicate with these specialists and coordinate their communications with one another.

## REVIEW

In hiring an outside consultant, what precautions should you take?

How can you stay up to date on labor legislation, interpretations, and court decisions?

Name the steps to set up a master accounting system for a company.

What activities are normally included in industrial engineering?

# 15

# MANAGING A SMALL BUSINESS

The manager of a small business faces most of the problems of a large one. At the outset many of these problems are not apparent, but eventually most of them will appear, especially as the company grows. The functions and problems of a large business are shared by many managers, each one specializing in a given area of the business. On the other hand, the functions and problems of a small business are managed by one or, at most, a few persons. So greater versatility is required of the manager of a small business. Usually longer hours, too.

## DEFINITIONS

The Small Business Act defines "small business" as "one which is independently owned and operated and not dominant in its field of operation." The Committee for Economic Development (CED) defines "small business" in terms of four criteria:

1. The management is independent; usually the managers are also owners.
2. Capital and ownership are held by one or a small group of individuals.
3. Operations are local although markets need not be.
4. The company is relatively small for its industry.

Some writers draw a distinction between an individual in business for himself, perhaps with an office assistant, and small business. It's difficult to draw the line. As soon as the individual hires another person has he become a small business? Take, for example, a TV and radio repairman. He hires someone to take telephone calls and handle the office work. As the business grows, he hires another repairman. Whereas at one time he operated from his garage, he finally rents a small shop. The business continues to grow, and he takes on the sale of radio and TV sets. At the urging of TV manufacturers, he stocks standard parts. Then he has to assign one of the shop assistants to handle the stockroom. By this time he is certainly a small businessman and has begun to encounter most of the problems which arise in any business.

The manager of a small business wears many hats. He must keep up to date in his field. In addition, he needs to broaden his background in accounting, finance, marketing, psychology, sociology, office practices, and economics.

Dentists, doctors, professional engineers, management consultants, and other professionals or paraprofessionals can scarcely be considered small businessmen for our purposes. They have special problems which will not be considered here. We have in mind businesses like the following: baking, dry cleaners, restaurants, automobile service, cabinetmaking. To this group of producers should be added retail stores, dealerships, and wholesalers. Any of these may employ scores of persons.

## How to Offset Risks

Managers of small businesses face many pitfalls. To offset some of the risks, the following points need to be considered:

*Experience in the line of work.* Knowledge alone may not be enough. Knowledge supported by experience can be a prime ingredient for success. As the business grows, it may be possible to hire individuals who bring to the business additional, specialized knowledge or experience. But for one individual to assume the management of a small business without having both attributes is extremely risky.

*Planning.* Plans should be in writing. At the outset, short-term goals of a few months or a year should be set. Later, longer-range planning can be started.

*Capital, particularly working capital.* Typical drains on initial capital are granting too much credit, investing too heavily in capital goods, and hiring too many employees before this is justified by sales. Another expenditure that guarantees failure is for the owner-manager to draw too-high salary or expenses, which drains working capital from his infant business.

## Other Problems of Small Businesses

Many small businesses attempt to produce too many products or offer too many services. Output should be limited to products and services within the competence of the management. Even large companies have come to grief for trying to offer too many products.

Failure to balance production with marketing has been a problem with many small businesses. Often they have been started by mechanically or technically experienced individuals who are interested in production but not in sales. If goods can't be moved, inventory piles up and working capital is tied up. On the other hand, if sales and orders get ahead of production, the condition can usually be remedied by hiring more people, setting up a second shift, or working overtime. No small business can ignore its marketing problems.

In the beginning the owner-manager of a small business is likely to spend many hours trying to keep things going. He must do the lowly tasks as well as the important ones. In this way, he acquires confidence in quite a few areas. Unfortunately, as he hires new people he may fail to delegate to them and so may make poor use of his and his subordinates' time. Poor use of managerial time limits chances for growth and success in small businesses even more than it does in large companies.

To learn how to use time more effectively, some managers have found it helpful to keep a detailed log of everything they do in a given week—telephone calls, interviewing, dictating, clerical activities, production, selling, and so on. At the end of the sample week they analyze their activities. The log helps them plan their activities better and make more efficient schedules and pinpoints duties to be delegated. Keeping a log is an excellent exercise for managers in companies of any size.

The owner-manager of a small business runs into many of the same problems of employee relationships as managers in big companies. These problems include selecting employees, wages, training, supervision, fringe benefits, turnover, and the like. Many of these problems do not surface right away, but as the business grows they inevitably will.

The managers of small businesses are caught on the horns of a dilemma. They should use as much specialized outside help as they can get—lawyers, market researchers, tax advisers, financiers, accountants, management consultants, and others. On the other hand, working capital is so limited that they cannot afford to pay much for such outside help. Here the information and advisory sources listed in the previous chapter may be useful.

Little noticed in the field of management are the problems of nonprofit cooperatives. Most are marketing co-ops but they may embrace group purchasing, member training, and counseling. Usually, elected directors appoint a manager who hires whatever help is needed and supervises activities, including accounting. Other than their nonprofit organizational setup and financing, their management problems are like those of any business.

## Equipment Leasing

One way that a small businessman can get the advantage of good capital equipment, yet avoid heavy capital investment, is to use equipment leasing. For small companies, leasing may be the only way to get equipment that will let them compete with large companies.

Leasing offers many benefits to the equipment user. Since ownership stays with the lessor, he usually carries maintenance costs. If equipment becomes obsolete, the lessee isn't saddled with that cost. Whereas buying equipment calls for heavy cash outlays, leasing does not, so working capital is conserved. When leased equipment is no longer needed, the lessor handles its disposition or salvage.

Leasing offers access to credit for new equipment which a small businessman might otherwise not be able to get. Leased equipment is not shown as an asset nor does it create a liability on the balance sheet, though an independent auditor may require that a footnote be added to the financial statements if the lease is a long-term, substantial one. So, the lessee will show a stronger financial position and still have the equipment he needs.

Companies which already own expensive equipment assets may find advantages in finding a purchaser for these assets and then leasing them back. This releases cash for working capital purposes.

Rentals normally cover a period of one year or less; leases, normally more than a year. A payout lease will recover for the lessor the cost of equipment plus interest, administrative expense, and profit. A nonpayout lease recovers something less, and the lessor will eventually take back the equipment to re-lease it or to sell it. This practice is often used where asset durability is high, such as where materials handling or computer equipment is involved.

## FRANCHISES

In recent decades, franchising has become an important way for people to go into business for themselves. The person taking a franchise should have some experience in the same field of business. Most franchisers supply training, operating manuals, help in site selection, building design, and sometimes aid in franchising. A franchiser sets up all elements of a standardized business which is to be operated by a franchisee and teaches him how to run it.

After a franchise is in operation, the franchiser may provide field supervision, inspection, and sales promotion assistance. Sometimes national advertising, employee training, and centralized purchasing are included. A franchise contract should spell out in detail the obligations of both parties—financial, quality of product or service, advertising, territory, sources of supply, and so on. The manager of a franchise operation should insist on all possible support from the other party to his contract.

Franchising was oversold in the 1960s and early 1970s as a means of achieving the great dream of being one's own boss. Many abuses by franchisers have been discovered. As a result, there is a lot more regulation of franchises and more information on the subject is available than ever before. Before investing in a franchise, the businessman should carefully examine every aspect of the opportunity. This should include directing inquiries to the state attorney general.

## SUCCESS IN A SMALL BUSINESS

Although many problems of a small businessman are similar to those encountered by managers of larger organizations, the success factors reveal important degrees of difference. Selecting the right kind of business at the right time may be half the battle. Riding a rising trend has been responsible for many great successes.

One way to spot an emerging trend is to study newspaper want ads for the past year or two. When these show increasing needs for certain types of new jobs or certain new industries, this is one indicator of a growth trend. Other signs are newspaper articles about some new product or service, attractiveness to young employees, ready financing by government or financial institutions, and established corporations gobbling up small businesses which now offer the product or service.

To spot an emerging movement consider the opportunities opened up by other easily identified trends: population changes, suburban growth, changing life-styles, new legislation, new transportation needs, new equipment needs, changing popular attitudes.

## SMALL-BUSINESS FINANCE

Lack of adequate financing can deal a fatal blow to a new small enterprise. Equipment leasing can lessen capital needs, but working capital is needed for rent, supplies, payroll, and other expenses. Suppliers are less likely to allow 90 or 120 days credit to small businesses than to large. Very few banks will grant loans to small businesses without substantial collateral. Large businesses usually have large lines of credit at their banks. Venture capital may be available if a new company looks particularly promising. But even here, venture capitalists prefer companies or individuals with proven track records. Such records are usually found among large companies and successful businessmen.

How you organize a small business is not so important at the outset but assumes greater importance if the company grows fast.

The advantages of incorporating are not as great for small businesses as they are for big. Legal advice is needed on timing the transition from proprietorship to partnership to corporation.

The selection of each new employee for a small business is more important than for a large corporation. Since he will probably handle many duties, he has "job enrichment" from the beginning. Small businesses usually can't offer a full range of security and fringe benefits. This makes it difficult to compete with large companies for hired help. As an offset, small businesses offer more interesting work than large; friendly relations with fellow employees and greater opportunity for recognition.

For companies that sell products, procurement is important. Sources of supply must be firm, preferably with liberal credit terms. But small businesses with less buying power compared to large are at a disadvantage. Small businesses do not have the resources to give them a chance to choose between making a component or buying it. Their options on make-buy decisions are limited. General Motors can decide whether to buy shock absorbers, make them, or buy a company which makes them. A small company has no such option.

Recordkeeping is important. Because of the expense involved, the advantages of computers were once limited to big companies. Fortunately, computerized recordkeeping is now offered by data processing service bureaus, so this gap is not as wide today as it was a few years ago.

In addition to the bigger buying power large companies have, they also have more selling muscle. The small business must learn to sell smarter, to carve out a niche for itself by giving more personal attention and service to customers.

## Professional Corporations for the Self-Employed

Some self-employed and highly successful people such as doctors, lawyers, athletes, and actors have incorporated themselves or formed professional corporations. For a long time the Internal Revenue Service looked with a jaundiced eye on such incorporations but finally had to accept them after losing several important court decisions.

A professional corporation may have many advantages, including tax deductible group life insurance, sick pay, health insurance, death benefits, and profit sharing plans. Self-incorporation or forming a professional corporation is subject to so many changes, new tax rulings and decisions, that professional advice is essential. Top-notch legal, tax, and accounting advice are needed. Changes in these areas occur so rapidly that no book about them can be current.

Another tax advantage to the self-employed is offered by the Keogh Plan, which allows tax deductions for contributions made to a personal retirement fund. Appreciation of funds invested in the plan and income from it are not currently taxed. Funds cannot be withdrawn from the plan at will, however: Many banks and most mutual funds can provide detailed information about this retirement plan for self-employed individuals. Like self-incorporation, details of the Keogh Plan are subject to change. Professional legal, tax, and accounting advice are needed for the latest information available.

Most people would rather work for a corporation than undertake the risks of being in business for themselves. For them a regular pay check and the security of employment are all-important. Small companies are subject to severe blows in times of recession. Moreover, they normally lack the fringe benefits that are offered by large organizations. The hours of work for managers of small companies are likely to be much longer than if they were doing similar work for a large corporation. Staff assistance is lacking, so that the manager must do many menial chores or pick up information from different sources. Many small businesses are family owned and operated, and a competent manager may find himself overruled, or confronted with some member of the family who knows little about the problems.

On the other hand, big corporations can be soul-less. Sometimes a manager feels that he is so far away from the fountainhead of decisions that he is nothing more than a pawn in the corporate game. Moreover, he may miss the warm friendships which frequently develop in a small company. Each person must study his fundamental needs to determine whether they will be met best in the shelter of a corporation or in the hot seat of running a small business.

## REVIEW

How would you define a small business?

Name at least four pitfalls faced by a small businessman.

What are some benefits of equipment leasing?

Name at least three franchise operators in your community.

Name five or more factors which make for the success of a small business.

What are some benefits of the Keogh Plan?

# 16

# BUSINESS AND SOCIAL ACCOUNTABILITY

Recent decades have witnessed a marked tendency for business to be blamed for many of society's ailments. Many profound statements have been made about the responsibilities of business to society. But little is heard about the obligations of various segments of society to business—society's productive arm.

When social schemes fail, legislators use business as a whipping boy. At the same time, they levy increasing tribute in the form of taxes upon producers, thus limiting the fertility of the goose that lays the golden eggs.

Education should prepare each upcoming generation for productive citizenship, not just for more education. Perhaps greater use should be made of the "half classroom, half employment" plan for college and even the last year of high school. Some educators, who have never had to meet a payroll, attack the very system which makes their livelihoods possible.

Unions seem to believe that employers have an inexhaustible pot of gold for higher wages, failing to realize that without increased worker productivity, the gold soon becomes wasted by inflation. Working *with* management, unions could be a potent force in our nation's well-being.

In no way do the derelictions of various segments of society relieve business of its own responsibilities. On the other hand, business should not be blamed for the errors of legislators, of economic advisers to the federal government, of starry-eyed theorists, or of shortsighted union leaders. Organized business provides most of the products and services needed for a viable economy.

## Prophets of Doom

Much of the undeserved criticism of business comes from misconceptions held by the prophets of doom. They look back with nostalgia to "the good old days" when America was young, and they condemn many of the innovations of modern living. Let's consider some of the facts.

A century and a half ago, the life span in the United States was short; on the average, males lived 38 years. Employees worked from sunup to sundown, sometimes seven days a week. Average pay was perhaps $25 a month. Housewives didn't have dishwashers, vacuum cleaners, or automatic refrigerators. Food was monotonous and scarce. There was no central heating for homes, and the only rooms with adequate heating in winter were those with a fireplace. No one had even dreamed of air conditioning. Epidemics of various diseases were rampant. The travel of most individuals was confined to 25 or 30 miles from home. Against that "good old days" backdrop, contrast the life of the average citizen today in any developed nation.

Prophets of doom, usually zealous and frequently misguided, tend to blame industry unjustly for a lot of situations. For example, during World War II a powerful insecticide known as "DDT" was developed. In less than a decade, insect-borne diseases such as malaria, yellow fever, and typhus were sharply reduced all over the world. At the same time, food production increased in many nations and famines became rarer. Between the reduction of disease and the increase of available food, DDT can be credited with saving the lives of millions of individuals.

In the early 1960s, the prophets of doom, pointing out that DDT had killed some fish and some birds, became a disaster lobby. They pressured the U.S. government, which banned the use of DDT. Soon other countries followed suit. The results are that malaria is on the rise, food production in many countries has decreased, and famine once more rears its ugly head. Gypsy moths, as an example, are once again destroying our forests. In some countries, laws against DDT have been repealed because of the obvious need for this insecticide. Worldwide the opponents of DDT have probably been unwittingly responsible for millions of deaths!

This instance is cited to illustrate how a vocal minority with the best intentions but without full information, can prevent the advancement of mankind by criticizing private enterprise. Opposition to nuclear power plants is preventing electric utilities from supplying adequate power. In situations like these, mankind is faced with trade-off alternatives: DDT or famine, atomic energy production or electric blackouts. Were it not for industry the choices would not exist.

No one has proven that the bigger the business, the more it harms the public interest. Nevertheless government regularly goes about breaking up big business in the United States. Many advanced foreign governments encourage increasing size while still restraining use of monopoly power. This fact undoubtedly accounts for some of the clout of foreign competition in world trade.

## Ever Bigger Government

Statistics attest to the burgeoning of government, whether federal, state, or local. The percentage of each dollar of personal income in the United States resulting from direct government payments—wages, welfare, social security, and the like—is rising. State and local governments are growing at an even faster rate than the federal government.

The oligarchies of ancient Greece were based on the belief that their members were superior to the common people. The same belief is surfacing again among people in government. There is a drift toward centralized governmental control. But if governments feel themselves superior, then the will of the people is likely to be thwarted by the legislators, by the courts, or by officials, both elected and appointed. There is great danger in looking to government for the solution to all social problems.

Unfortunately, it is unlikely that the drift toward oligarchy and centralized government can be readily halted. Management in the future has few options. It can strongly oppose the drift; it can knuckle under to it, becoming another servant of the State; or it can become more active in social change, forming a partnership for progress with government.

Management must take a large share of the blame for the criticism and legal constraints which are aimed at business. While legislators, union leaders, and social do-gooders have damned business, the tendency of managers has been to suffer in silence, instead of showing people the benefits they derive from the business system. In addition, except for a handful of outstanding business leaders, management has not considered social responsibilities as an obligation. Managers have thought of themselves as responsible to their stockholders first. Modernization of personnel policies has improved the sense of responsibility to employees. Still, consumers, environment, and society in general have been subordinated in management's thinking. This attitude is changing but needs to change at a more rapid pace.

## Major Criticisms of Business

Public opinion surveys reveal negative attitudes toward business and considerable ignorance. Most people believe that big corporations make exorbitant profits. They also believe that profits fail to result in better goods and services. They do not understand why profits are needed for expansion and research and as an essential ingredient for the development of a higher standard of living. Several surveys of college students also show that most of them are convinced that management is little concerned with profits for social welfare, that it is mainly concerned with profits for stockholders.

Business is often criticized for polluting the environment—air, water, and land resources. More recently, the term "pollution" has been broadened to include the bad effects of noise. Business is criticized for placing stockholder interests above social welfare.

Poor corporate performance comes in for much adverse comment. This indictment includes misleading advertising, poor product quality, planned obsolescence, and lack of service. Another concern is unfair distribution of corporate income. This includes low wages to women and minority workers, price fixing, and overly generous benefits to major executives. One need not agree with these viewpoints, but he must accept the fact that they exist in the minds of a great many people.

Against these indictments, some companies are undertaking long-range planning for social responsibilities. Their plans include (1) better attention to employee needs, (2) greater involvement of employees in goal setting, (3) more participation in community activities, (4) more policies designed to protect consumers and to insure quality products, (5) better service, (6) more cooperation with government in attempting to meet social problems, and (7) more honesty in advertising and in telling consumers what products will and will not do.

The United States has 6 percent of the world's population but contributes 40 percent of its pollution. The pollution problem has become foremost in the public consciousness over the last decade. Air, land, and water pollution provide headaches for many communities. Municipal, state, and federal governments are themselves often flagrant offenders. Managers of both public and private institutions are being pressured to find solutions for a deteriorating environment.

Some steps have already been taken: Paper, glass, and metal are being recycled. Sewage treatment plants are being built. Controls of offshore oil rigs are more stringent. Purification of manufacturing effluent, and noise and smoke abatement controls have been instituted. In many ways the environment is being protected. While the impetus for such steps has come from special groups, management has taken note and must build such controls into all planning.

Industrial nations have been built by emphasizing more production regardless of its effects on the environment. Environmentalists want to accent the *quality* of life so that man enjoys his world without debasing it. Combining these needs with a necessity to conserve raw materials and other natural resources will challenge management leadership in the foreseeable future.

## Corporate Responsibility

The scope of corporate responsibility to society has never been clearly defined. However, each passing decade enlarges it. Society has a right to expect responsible corporate behavior to include:

Product quality.
Product safety.
Prices which yield a reasonable profit.
Honest sales promotion.
Jobs which interest, challenge, and develop workers.
Avoidance of race, color, creed, or sex discrimination in selection and promotion.
Employee health and safety.
Retirement income for long-service employees.
Payment of a minimum wage to unskilled workers and a fair wage to those above the lowest level.
Payment of a fair share of taxes.
Protection of the environment.

All of the above items provide good examples of scope enlargement. None of these items would have been considered a corporate responsibility to society at the turn of the century. Some of them were not considered responsibilities only a few years ago. New responsibilities will be added to this list. That will be a continuing trend.

Advocates of even greater social responsibility on the part of business managers believe that profits and productivity stem from proper corporate actions. They say that society cannot allow business to pollute, to plunder natural resources, to make false advertising claims, to build planned obsolescence into products, or to destroy worker initiative with boring tasks.

In addition to financial reports, present managers have to account to government regulatory agencies for taxes; wages; hours; and employee health, working conditions, and safety. Future managers may well have to keep records on contributions to community and national well-being such as education, environment, use of resources, and participation in social or political activities.

The term "social accounting" has come into the language of management. Some companies in their annual reports to stockholders report progress in safety, employee health measures, insurance, pensions, minority employment, advancement of female employees, charitable contributions, and community assistance. In this way, they are educating shareholders to accept spending for social ends.

Business today functions in a different socioeconomic climate than that which existed less than a decade ago. Wise managers will not try to hold back the tide flooding toward greater corporate social responsibility. Indeed, they will be unable to do so.

## Social Accounting

Increasingly, standards of conduct are being determined for management rather than by management. Laws and public opinion suggest that society does not believe business can police itself against ruthlessness, harmful products, labor exploitation, destruction of natural resources, pollution, deceptive advertising, excessive profits, and other faults laid at its door.

Social standards and customs are in a constant state of change. If management genuinely means to meet its social responsibilities it must look ahead, not lag behind. Forecasts of social demands belong in management's long-range planning.

Many big companies in their annual reports describe the *money* they have spent on pollution control, hiring minorities, promoting women, consumer protection, and other social benefits. Unfortunately, rarely has management of a big company been the leader in these moves. For the most part they have been forced upon business by legislation and public demand.

Some business leaders are finally awakening to the idea of corporate social responsibility. For example the Xerox Corporation has in effect a "social service leave program." Under this plan an employee may receive up to a year's leave at full pay to pursue some worthwhile community project. An evaluation committee studies proposed projects and recommends the names of individuals who should be granted such leaves of absence.

Some companies are offering financial and managerial assistance to minority businesses. Some are sponsoring public service broadcasts or television documentaries in the public interest. Others are joining hands with educational institutions in order to promote research or to train individuals in necessary skills. Some are taking an active part in residential and commercial development of central city areas. A few are adopting a system which has been in effect in Europe for many years, namely, day-care centers for children of employees. Some companies are setting up educational programs aimed at drug abuse, gang warfare, pollution, or even political corruption.

Any company that seriously plans to enlarge its social responsibilities can profit by following these guidelines:

- ☐ The top executive must be committed—not just sold.
- ☐ A high-level executive must be designated to look for service opportunities and to keep the program moving.
- ☐ Activities must be kept flexible.
- ☐ A continuing program of training and upgrading minority employees must be followed.
- ☐ Communication channels must be kept open with employees and civic leaders.
- ☐ Many employees must be involved in the program.
- ☐ Other companies should be brought into the effort.

Some corporate social planners looking into the future believe that more than corporate money is needed. Corporate leadership and human resources cannot be bought with money; they must be made available to communities. Great business leaders will have to apply the operational skills of corporate leadership to the major problems of society.

## The Employer Compliance Maze

One of the most difficult parts of managing today is to insure that policies and practices are in compliance with the laws relating to labor relationships. Most laws have resulted in executive orders, administrative interpretations, and regulations pertaining to collective bargaining, equal employment opportunities, fair employment practices, and occupational health and safety standards. Many nations have laws regulating severance, vacations, and other conditions of employment. In addition to federal laws on these subjects there are state and sometimes local laws. Sometimes these are in conflict.

In some instances, an employer is caught in the middle of a conflict between a federal and a state law. For example, certain state laws restrict the number of hours a female employee can work in a day, but in some instances this may run counter to federal anti-discrimination laws.

In this jungle of regulations an employer finds it difficult to keep up with the latest laws, interpretations, and decisions. Moreover, he may find it difficult to alter his own personnel practices and policies in conformity. He has several options:

1. He can carry on as at present, ignoring changes in laws and regulations, and hope for the best. It may come as a costly shock to find decisions against him.

2. He may employ a personnel manager who is well versed in labor laws and assign to him the task of keeping up with changing rules and regulations. Such an individual will have to question present personnel policies and practices and will often run into the opposition of line managers who resent his interference.

3. He can keep in touch with all developments himself. To assist him in this there are various loose-leaf and indexed services to which he can subscribe. Or he may retain the services of a competent outside personnel consultant.

Good pay and intentions on an employer's part are not sufficient to keep him out of trouble. Excellent records are essential. Also, employers at least once a year should review all personnel practices and policies to make certain that they still conform to the laws. Working through the employer compliance maze is becoming an increasingly important part of the job of major executives.

## OSHA

This is the familiar term for the Occupational Safety and Health Act. The act says that "each employer shall furnish to each of his employees, employment and place of employment which are free from recognized hazards that are causing or are likely to cause death or serious physical harm to his employees."

The law provides many standards for plant safety. The most common violations so far found have been faulty scaffolding, dangerous and careless storage of combustibles, electrical problems, inadequate guards on machinery, excessive noise, poor ventilation, noxious fumes, absence of in-plant health facilities, and hazards peculiar to a particular industry—construction, for example—or to a particular job, such as working with radium.

is to ask his insuring company to provide plant inspection. Any

The safest way for an employer to avoid heavy fines under OSHA insurance company which has been insuring for plant liability and property will have experience in safety and health. Eliminating as many hazards as possible is a form of protection for the insurance company itself. Safety inspection can assure compliance with the law and might bring about reductions in accidents.

The Riegel Products Corporation of Milford, New Jersey, has cut lost time injuries in half by a well-planned safety program. The program calls for top management support, acceptance of OSHA as a "partner in safety," continuing indoctrination of management and supervisory personnel, and effective communications with employees, especially from supervisors. The company safety director believes that emphasis on the human aspects of the safety problem is largely responsible for the program's success.

Looking to the future, it seems likely that some form of national health plan will be passed. Such a plan would require employers to provide health insurance for employees and their families. Several proposals for legislation along these lines have already been made, and is seems probable that one of them will ultimately become law.

The commission created by the Consumer Product Safety Act has powers to set safety standards for thousands of products. It can ban, seize, or recall items; require safety certification; inspect manufacturing operations; subpoena records; levy fines; and seek criminal penalties for violations. All managers need to be alert to the implications of this law.

## Government Aids

Government gives as well as takes. Few managers take advantage of the wealth of data available from federal and state governments. The departments of Commerce, Labor, Interior, Defense, and Agriculture issue periodic reports of interest to business managers, mainly through various bureaus, such as the bureaus of Census, Standards, and Mines.

In addition, certain agencies and commissions supply data of possible interest. Typical are the Federal Reserve Board, Export-Import Bank, Interstate Commerce Commission, Securities and Exchange Commission, and the Federal Trade Commission. A booklet from the Government Printing Office, in Washington, lists hundreds of government publications of interest to managers and useful in advancing business social accountability.

## REVIEW

What are some of the differences between the "good old days" of 150 years ago and today?

Name some major criticisms frequently leveled at business.

What kinds of behavior does society expect of business corporations?

What does the term "social accounting" mean?

What is OSHA?

Name some departments of the federal government which issue publications of interest to businessmen.

# 17

# MANAGEMENT IN THE YEARS AHEAD

Forecasting is risky business. If time proves the forecaster wrong, he becomes the object of ridicule. If he is right, people say his predictions were obvious.

In December 1959, *Newsweek, Reader's Digest,* and other magazines peered ahead to 1970. They envisioned a relatively tranquil world. The United States and the Soviet Union would lose their dominant positions, and Red China would attack Taiwan. There would be disarmament, a federal budget of $120 billion, and a gross national product of $700 billion. They also forecast the end of grimy tenements, of congested cities, and of air pollution; the introduction of family helicopters and of worldwide transportation of mail by rockets; and a return to Victorian decencies. Finally, *Newsweek* suggested, "For the tourist who really wants to get away from it all—safaris in Vietnam."

None of these predictions was valid by 1970. Hopefully, a similar fate will not befall the predictions in this chapter on the future of the national economy, social change, government, and management.

## THE NATIONAL ECONOMY

The national economy is extraordinarily complex. Parts of the economy grow at different rates just as various companies and industries do. Certain regions of our country make faster progress than others. The best single index of the national economy is the gross national product (GNP).

A simple definition of "gross national product" is the total market value of all the goods and services a country has produced in a given year. For the United States, the GNP has increased at an accelerating pace. For example, in the three decades following 1941, it rose from $100 billion to approximately $1 trillion. This end result was more than a mere multiplication by ten, because the structural mix was different—for example, services became a larger portion of the total.

This fact has been both cause and effect. As more and more families passed subsistence levels, they had discretionary income which could be spent for more tangibles, or for more services—greater education for children, beauty parlors, recreation, transportation, telephone, electricity, government facilities, insurance, and more. These demands in turn have diverted employees to service jobs, contributing to labor shortage problems in manufacturing. At the same time, demands for services have created new management jobs in the many service industries. The trend will continue as the percentage of poverty-level families decreases.

Moreover, some of the tenfold increase in GNP resulted, and continues to result, from inflation. The *real* GNP (that is, discounted for inflation) over the three decades may have multiplied perhaps only six times. Increases in productivity, resulting principally from wise capital investment, obviously add to the standard of living. Price inflation, however, presents managers with complex decisions resulting from higher costs for raw materials, labor, capital funds, and marketing. These costs must be offset by price increases consistent with sales competition, government regulations, and consumer disposition of income. Since inflation will continue, managers of the future must pay increasing attention to its many effects on their operations.

The principal contributors to a trillion-dollar economy and the appropriate percentages of their contributions are:

| | |
|---|---|
| Manufacturing | 28% |
| Wholesale and retail trade | 17% |
| Finance, insurance, and real estate | 13% |
| Government enterprises | 13% |

| | |
|---|---|
| Services | 11% |
| Agriculture, forestry, fisheries, mining, construction, etc. | 10% |
| Transportation, communication, gas and electric, utilities, etc. | 8% |
| | 100% |

Of these seven principal contributors to the economy, the manufacturing percentage is likely to decrease due not to lower output but to the increasing importance of the other elements, with the possible exception of agriculture. The outlook enhances the likelihood that managerial opportunities in service activities will outstrip those in manufacturing.

The long-term growth rate of GNP may be as much as 4 percent per annum. However, cyclical swings in business activity will accelerate or decelerate this growth temporarily. Some forces at work tend to lessen growth; others tend to augment it. Those which might detract from a 4 percent growth rate are increasing taxes, shorter work weeks, the shifting of workers from manufacturing to services, and increasing employment by governments. Factors contributing to growth are an increase in the labor force with a fairly stable rate of unemployment, greater expenditures for research and capital goods, more use of automation, governmental support of production, and dynamic management. Balancing out the detractors versus the contributors, the net result will be a continuing increase in gross national product, which will, however, include a troublesome increase in inflation. Living standards (real growth in goods and services) will rise.

Scientists of many kinds have made tremendous contributions to our standard of living. Most of the physical scientists and engineers who have ever lived are alive today. In science what's past is but prologue to the tremendous advances which are on the drawing boards, in the test tubes, or beginning to develop in the dreams of creative scientists. No one can foresee all the changes that scientific discovery will bring about. But even those on the horizon seem destined to continue the recent acceleration of science and technology.

Economists expect rather slow growth in some of the basic industries, such as lumber, mining, coal, leather, iron, and steel. On the other hand, great growth is expected in industries producing machinery, instruments, chemicals, plastics, and electric power. The fast-growing manufacturing industries are obviously tied in with productivity, automation, and computerization. Electronic data processing is rapidly being adopted by some service activities such as banking, utilities, insurance, government, and the military. However, many service industries are highly personalized and unaffected by technological innovations.

A growing and better-educated labor force, a burgeoning technology, greater capital investment, and more sophisticated management form a synergism, that is, the whole effect is greater than the sum of its parts. This statement is true largely because of the leadership integration provided by management. The future manager must coordinate information from both internal and external sources in short- and long-range planning which will necessarily include many important decisions implied in this book.

## SOCIAL CHANGE

The harbingers of rapid change are all around us. They show in social unrest and radicalism. There has been alienation from traditional customs, and resistance to "the establishment." The puritan ethic no longer influences attitudes toward work. Individualism has always been an important underpinning of capitalism, but this has shifted to its extreme form—egocentrism. While scientific advances have always run into opposition, nuclear power has produced a vague queasiness—an inability to oppose on solid grounds of self-interest and self-protection.

Another evidence of social change is increasing consciousness of the importance of natural resources and environment. Whereas political, industrial, financial, educational, and religious leadership once was respected, current social change has brought deep distrust. In the twenty-first century, it may well be that these fires of discontent will destroy the existing social order.

Some sociologists believe that we are at the Great Divide between the industrial society and a "post-industrial" technological future. Millions of people will have to face tremendous changes in jobs and status. This torrent of change will undoubtedly affect industry. Some managers feel so threatened by the pace of change that they resist it, or even deny its existence. Their collision with the oncoming future will prove painful.

The post-industrial era will be service-oriented, will emphasize professional and technical personnel, will amass knowledge on a worldwide scale, will plan innovations, growth, and the direction of scientific inquiry, will rely on computerized solutions to complex social problems and analyses of trends. Characteristic of such a future will be less emphasis on work, economic advancement, and business efficiency. Accented will be widespread education, acceptance of accelerating social change, leisure activities, and pursuit of individualistic aims. These changes will sweep over the highly industrialized nations first.

Adaptive managers will keep an open mind toward social change, even to the point of leading an obvious trend. For example, the large First Pennsylvania Bank of Philadelphia publicly announced goals for hiring, promoting, lending to, and buying from minority groups. Later it reported on both its successes and failures. The company's president, James F. Bodine, says, "It's a fallacy that corporate responsibility is contrary to the profit motive. . . ."

Some measurable manifestations of accelerating change are goods produced, rates of travel, power consumed, and speed of communication. These figures have been doubling every 15 years.

The information explosion is largely responsible for technological innovation. The computer, through its vast power for storage and integrating knowledge, speeds up the innovative process to yield new products and new processes, as well as new knowledge. Managers of the future will themselves seek computer applications and will not merely rely on staff specialists, who may understand computers but not broad-scope management.

Social change has not kept pace with technological change. Subcultures have not been absorbed into the mainstream. Nature's resources are still being exploited with no thought for tomorrow. The gap between have and have-not nations (subgroups, too) widens. Education largely trains for the vanishing past rather than for the onrushing future. Industry lags behind public opinion and social legislation.

In no sense is discontent confined to the United States or to workers in production. Virtually all advanced nations are suffering much the same unrest. It is reaching into office staffs, government workers, and other knowledge workers, and even into the managerial levels. Boredom, absenteeism, labor turnover, poor quality of work, alcoholism, and drug addiction are global phenomena. Worldwide, managers need to consider research findings of sociologists, psychologists, demographers, and anthropologists. They need to match their acceptance of these social scientists with their acceptance of physical scientists.

The newly emerged nations, as well as established low-economy nations, are astir with rising expectations. More than a century ago, the French historian Alexis de Tocqueville wrote, "The evil which was suffered patiently as inevitable seems unendurable as soon as the idea of escaping from it crosses men's minds."

However, the nations of the world simply do not have the capital, the know-how, or the natural resources to satisfy the expectations of all the people of all the nations. If international stability is to be realized, managers everywhere must play a leading role in setting *realistic* economic goals and in providing the needed leadership to achieve them.

World population continues to accelerate. In many nations and particularly in the less developed ones, population growth is winning the race against productivity. In 1798, the English economist Thomas Malthus advanced the theory that population tends to increase faster than food supply, with wars, famines, or other catastrophes as the inevitable result. The decades ahead may well witness a real test of the Malthusian theory. Managers, by producing and distributing foodstuffs (especially proteins), may well avert Armageddon. It is beyond their scope as managers to take a position on limitation of population.

In the United States, by 1980, the fastest growing age group will be between the ages of 20 and 29, which condition will increase the labor force. Managers already are having to adjust to younger employees, their ideals, life-styles, and work ethic. The work force may well be 100 million people.

People will be clustered in dense megalopolises, which arise from the union of the great industrial communities. For example, "Boswash" may include all communities from Boston to Washington. Even now 80 percent of Americans live on an elbow-jostling 2 percent of our land. Urban renewal efforts will likely prove insufficient to make cities more habitable. Hence, companies will increasingly locate plants and offices in suburban or rural areas, relying on local labor, providing supplementary transportation, and instituting flexible working hours.

In the decade ahead, industry will turn in an impressive performance. We shall see more high speed turbotrains, extended use of picture phones, ocean farming, cancer vaccine, new fabrics, synthetic foods, video home-education, multiple uses for lasers, numerous power sources, computerized shopping and banking. Real income of people, that is, their standard of living, will rise by at least 50 percent. To develop these innovations and make them available for general use, managers will need to risk investment, to set up production, to plan extensive marketing facilities, and to introduce new management practices.

"Ecology" is a relatively new word in society's lexicon. Protest alone will not eliminate air, water, soil, or noise pollution. Because public consciousness has been aroused, the outlook is excellent for ecological improvement. When individual citizens accept *their* responsibilities toward pollution, the problem will be considerably alleviated. Worldwide, governments and industry alike are tackling the problem.

We shall see better sewage treatment, quick disposal of oil slicks, "cleaner" internal-combustion engines, automobiles using fuel-cell power, more nuclear power, clean conversion of soft coal, some solar energy applications, noise abatement, smog control, and recycling of paper, glass, aluminum, and other solid wastes. Currently businesses are spending about $5 billion on solutions to pollution. All alert managers know that these ecological trends have already begun. Not all have tried to evaluate their long-term effects on their respective companies—costs, personnel and equipment needed, alterations in methods or products, and other effects.

The principal problems in the near future will be social rather than technological. Psychology, sociology, economics, and other social sciences will integrate to create *social engineering*, which future managers will study in colleges as they now study industrial engineering or business administration. Present managers can cover much the same ground through seminars and orientation offered by professional associations and other education programs. This is not the first generation to face change, nor will it be the last. An outstanding British statesman once said that each generation learns "to complain of the age we live in, to murmur at the present possessors of power, to lament the past, and to conceive extravagant hope for the future." The speaker was Edmund Burke; the year, 1792!

In summary, the decades ahead will be a period of disquiet. Since the momentum of existing trends cannot be retarded, the dawn of the future could already be history. Much of the control of that future lies in the hands of business and government leaders. These groups, entrusted with finding solutions to current and future problems, must realize that before they can find the right answers, they must ask the right questions. A decided force in future management will be the greater flow of information pertinent to the work of managers at all levels. The availability of extensive external and internal information will put a premium on the ability to ask the right question.

## GOVERNMENT

Governments, in general, contribute heavily to inflation and will continue to do so as long as they support the beyond-productivity demands of organized labor, since about 70 percent of the ultimate cost of goods is labor cost. In addition, governments contribute to the inflationary spiral by spending billions more than they take in and by issuing "printing press money." "Jawboning" of industry, plus price and profit controls, has never in the history of man succeeded in stopping inflation.

Government and political leaders will suffer from an ever-widening credibility gap. Strikes against government units will probably increase. Consumers will become more vocal. Concerned citizens will seek, and get, a larger voice in community affairs, local education, and environmental control, yet they will feel increasingly powerless in federal affairs. Lessening of parental authority will thrust disciplinary problems upon community governments, which are poorly equipped to handle such burdens.

In politics, moderation will temper both the extreme militant left and the extreme angry right. Public opinion will likely remain at the left of center. International tensions will remain and could easily inflame the great silent majority toward militancy.

Contributing to an era of conflict will be the rising levels of education, the creation of more jobs which require personal judgment, and the decline of autocratic authority. As people become disillusioned with federal remedies for urban sprawl, deteriorating cities, ghettos, the educational system, farm problems, and other ailments of society, we can expect a greater voice of protest and more mass action. Governments typically treat symptoms rather than diseases.

Even today, size in government is a problem. Frequently one agency issues regulations which impair or even completely oppose those of some other agency. There is much duplication of effort by governmental agencies, duplication of which they may not be aware. The problems of communication, so widespread in industry, are even greater among the many agencies of federal, state, and local governments. Unfortunately, the outlook is for a greater proliferation of agencies to meet upcoming problems rather than for a reduction.

In a period of lessened credibility toward established institutions (especially business), executives must either initiate a new leadership or become obedient servants of an autocratic state. To be effective, business leadership will tackle local social problems first. They will join foresighted leaders from government, service institutions, universities, and many branches of knowledge to provide coordinated direction to our society. Executives will take sabbatical leaves to handle government or social service posts. Social problems will be discussed by legislators whose numbers will include engineers, educators, doctors, social scientists, and business leaders, as well as lawyers. Utopia, maybe—but an achievable Utopia, if we want it badly enough!

A number of thoughtful scientists and economists are attempting to penetrate the future and to discover solutions to expected problems. These individuals and groups project current trends and construct mathematical models to illustrate the interrelationships among the factors at work; possible alternate futures are considered.

These economic seers are attempting to understand the processes at work which bring about change, and how they are interrelated. They contend that society's key resource is information, but that man does not know how to use the vast amount of information at his command. They believe that many problems are caused by obsolete institutions; some think that corporations, Congress, and other policy-making bodies are becoming obsolete. They believe that some of our social institutions are following practices and rules which were useful in the eighteenth and nineteenth centuries, but whose value has been outlived—practices good for survival but of little help in facing future problems. The values themselves are shifting as affluence is achieved in one country after another, bringing about changes in life-styles such as have already happened in the United States, the United Kingdom, and, to some extent, Canada.

In the United States alone there are over 400 independent research groups making studies in what has been called "futurology." Governments have created, or taken advantage of, existing "think tank" groups. One such is the Hudson Institute, located at Croton-on-Hudson, New York. It identifies important long-term trends, analyzes their principal components, makes projections, and attempts to predict the resulting world effects.

Typically a think tank consists of leading, highly specialized scientists of various disciplines who apply their knowledge to a given problem. In addition, science centers are being developed. An example is a nonprofit corporation, the University Science Center in Philadelphia, which is a consortium created by 27 colleges, universities, and medical schools. These supporters, and some 50 science-oriented tenants, have access to a giant computer in the Center. Science centers bring knowledge to bear on human problems. Government in the future will rely more and more on think tank groups and science centers to take advantage of their cumulative knowledge and expertise.

## MANAGEMENT IN THE FUTURE

The forces of change already discernible are so awesome that some writers believe we are in the midst of the second industrial revolution. Some people are apprehensive about the post-industrial era. Others rightly realize that these trends open up many career opportunities which will require more and better managers. Those who fail to come to grips with the management of change may face a change of management.

Likely future developments in industry and commerce will include:

- ☐ Growth of cybernetics, a term the dictionary defines as "the theoretical study of control processes in electronic, mechanical and biological systems, especially the mathematical analysis of the flow of information in such systems." This high-sounding definition can be simplified to mean "the study of the interrelationships between people and machines." In this context the word "people" includes employees, managers, and inventors; "machines" includes the environment and computers.

  Cybernetics is a much larger concept than simply linking men to machines or duplicating through machines. It includes concepts of total management information systems with feedback and repeated readjustments of policies and practices. Norbert Wiener, father of cybernetics, said that it embraced "the entire field of control and communication theory whether in the machine or the animal."
- ☐ Widespread application of computers to banking, credit, auditing, transportation, control of manufacturing processes, information storage, information retrieval, and other areas.
- ☐ Automated retail stores, accompanied by greater mass consumption.
- ☐ Extended uses for cryogenics, the science of low temperature phenomena ( − 100° and below). Examples are found in cryosurgery, human hibernation in medical treatments, cold working of metals, space research control of thermonuclear power, and preservation of whole blood.
- ☐ Widespread applications of lasers applied to metal working, worldwide communication, power transmission, radar, surgery, and military defense.
- ☐ New materials—high strength, high temperature superfabrics with special properties.
- ☐ Synthetic foods and beverages.
- ☐ More-rapid techniques in construction, mining, and earth moving. Examples: use of reinforced, premolded plastics; nuclear power in mining or tunneling and in oil extraction from shale.
- ☐ High capacity, worldwide communication.
- ☐ Declining importance of jobs in basic industries and in manufacturing.
- ☐ Increasing importance of service, professional, institutional, and governmental occupations, opening up more managerial opportunities in these areas.

Any predictions can, of course, be negated or reversed by cataclysmic events such as wars or famines, or by unexpected scientific discoveries.

Indicative of things to come is IBM's adaptation of a laser beam to scan packaged items at the checkout counter of a supermarket. The checker simply moves the symbol-marked items across the scanner while bagging the merchandise. The result is a list which prints out the items and prices, as well as the total. Other companies, such as National Cash Register and Sperry Rand, have developed their own supermarket checkout systems.

Another important technological development is miniaturized circuitry. A "chip" is an electronic memory device made of silicon, perhaps one-eighth inch in diameter, which replaces thousands of transistors. Microcomputers, the size of a book, already have the capacity of a much larger unit, at a tiny fraction of the cost. In the future virtually all businesses will either have their own computers or will rent time on a computer system that will serve as a quasi-public utility. Although some computers will be small enough to be held in the hand, they will have access to instant information through linkage with central data systems. The future will also see greater use of chips in cash registers, automobiles, home appliances, watches, and telephones. Every forward-looking manager will keep in touch with developments in this field of wizardry, seeking significant applications in his own business.

## Big Business Affects Managers

The welter of economic change described in this chapter will obviously have marked effect on future management. Bigness has brought affluence. It has also brought many problems. Government and industrial leaders are realizing that nations operating on the scale of the world's largest powers could destroy, or at least vitiate, the land, air, and water. Bigness has brought a feeling of alienation to many people. That same bigness cannot be reversed; indeed, it is like a snowball rolling downhill.

Managers must learn to deal with the problems which bigness has brought with it, and to see the opportunities which these problems present. They must repeatedly update their knowledge; study social trends, problems, and legislation; take an active, leading part in community activities, education, research, and solutions to housing, crime, pollution; disseminate information on the true benefits of the capitalist system; restore credibility through their actions and integrity.

In the past managers have been alert to growth; otherwise we would never have reached our present economic level. Managerial devices of planning, control, delegation, decentralization, mergers, and multinational organizations have not been results of growth—they have been the causes of growth, brought about by resourceful managers. But the time is overdue for a realization that managers must accept other values besides profit maximization and productivity. Social values have become obligations, not choices. At the same time, business managers and other leaders must realize that profits are essential if social responsibilities are to be met. A bankrupt company cannot be a good employer, a producer of good products or services, a good member of the community, and socially and environmentally responsible. Leadership in government and industry is at a premium as it has never been in any previous generation.

An old friend, Lawrence A. Appley, former chairman of the board of the American Management Associations, wrote me as follows: "A new kind of manager must evolve who can work with a group and consider himself, or herself, to be the recipient, analyzer, evaluator and utilizer of the skills, talents, experience and creativity of those who are working with him, or her, in the attainment of jointly arrived at objectives."

To an increasing extent, scientists, engineers, technicians, and managers are a mobile segment of our population. They accept jobs a thousand miles away, seeking higher income or more interesting positions. A giant corporation will transfer them from place to place, as they climb the executive ladder. The "brain drain" from Europe of highly trained men and women augments the picture of mobility.

Lately, however, some companies are meeting a countertrend. Their capable employees, especially the younger ones, are refusing promotions which require moving to distant points. Such refusals are in line with trends toward a new work ethic and toward self-fulfillment. Increasingly, managers will be "home grown" through executive development methods such as presented in this book.

While geographical movement among managers is declining, "executive obsolescence" is contributing to job mobility. Experience yields to knowledge in many kinds of managerial and professional work. Some executives, displaced and discouraged, turn to teaching, handicraft, or some totally different occupation—usually with a loss of income but often with higher personal satisfaction. Executive search agencies (sometimes dubbed "headhunters") further augment mobility in the higher echelons of management.

## Humanoid Robot Workers?

If a manufacturing operation can be described in minute detail, theoretically a machine can be made to perform it. The time is coming when much the same can be said about thought processes. For example, a chess player can now play chess with a computer-opponent. Electronic computers may give us androids, or humanoid robots, capable of performing many intricate tasks involving choice and decision. The possibility is already beyond the science fiction stage; hence managers must be alert to it.

Skepticism should be replaced by open-mindedness. After all, before most great inventions were proven practical, they were derided as useless or impossible. Should android workers come to pass, managers must be prepared to consider their many applications and their social implications.

Some gloomy Cassandras see Future Man as a faceless servant of the State—a number rather than a person, with Big Brother observing or directing his every move and thought. Others, more sanguine, see him as liberated from the monotony of routine tasks, his economic life secure, free to choose vocations and avocations from among many possibilities. If the latter prophecy proves true, it will result from the post-industrial Automation Age, which had its beginnings two or three decades ago.

## The Public Needs Economic Understanding

H. G. Wells, English historian (and a futurist before the word was invented) once said that humanity was in a race between education and catastrophe. Business managers, as an important segment of humanity, are active participants in that race. They face two distinct educational challenges:

1. Teaching the public how the free enterprise system works and how it made the United States the industrial leader of the world.
2. Developing future managers of industry and government to meet change.

The tools for widespread dissemination of economic knowledge are at hand—television, computer-assisted instruction, video tape, advertising, and the printed word. The missing ingredient is the awareness of business managers and government leaders that some such long-term program is needed in our national life to preserve our form of government and our position as one of the most advanced nations of the world.

In the future, manager training must include developing managers' abilities to educate the general public on the free enterprise system. Such training should go beyond typical graduate school courses in law, business regulation, finance, accounting, production, marketing, management, and organization. There must be greater accent on personnel problems, on human behavior, and on the social responsibilities of business to society. There must be more understanding by managers of the great significance of the worldwide availability of sheer information. Some graduate schools have started to include studies in social responsibility. Further expansion is needed.

It's accepted that engineers must periodically update themselves or become technically obsolete. The same can be said for managers. In an average business career of 40 years, a manager must continually update his business knowledge and upgrade his skills.

There are many hopeful signs. Quite a few big companies have set up their own management institutes. Some companies have in-plant audiovisual centers, hooked up with nearby universities. Some universities are taking an entirely new look at the problem of training business managers in the latest techniques of information systems, planning, control, finance, risk analysis, psychology, sociology, economics, and relations with government. It seems clear that more and more managers must retool their skills on the job, and that facilities must be made available to them so that they can adjust to change.

To decry the obvious fact that the social sciences have not kept pace with the physical sciences adds little to the nation's welfare. What needs development is means by which government and business leaders will be kept informed on advances in both areas.

In summary the managers of business and government in the future must see their tasks as part of the whole social structure, joining their respective contributions to keep society moving ahead.

## REVIEW

Define gross national product.

Name some harbingers of social change.

State two ways by which the federal government contributes to inflation.

Name a half-dozen future developments in commerce and industry.

What is your idea of an android worker?

Why should managers disseminate economic knowledge?

# 18

# PLANNING YOUR FUTURE

This is a chapter about *you*. It will consider the things you should *know* and *do* and *be* in order to meet the challenge of the future. Most of that challenge will be associated with bigness—of business, of government, of other institutions, and of problems. There will be big jobs to be filled, but if you are catapulted into such a job before you are ready for it, it may do you harm. The wound may heal but the scar will remain.

So this chapter will be devoted to pointing out ways to prepare yourself for a management job in the future—or, if you are already in such a job, ways to grow and take advantage of the vast changes which lie ahead.

Managers at all levels are younger and better educated than their predecessors. Some have obtained this education in college or graduate schools. Others have picked it up by studying along the way.

## What a Manager Should Know

You need to master far more than the technical knowledge required for operation of your department or business. The world faces some gigantic challenges, such as hunger, expanding population, shortages of materials and energy, pollution, fear of unknowns, and failure of the social sciences to keep pace with the physical sciences. Managers need to be statesmanlike in outlook if mankind is to rise above its own greed and stupidity.

## The Pressure of Rising Expectations

The peoples of the world seek higher standards of living. Newborn nations want the material goods enjoyed and earned by people in advanced countries. Expectations are rising the world over.

Some causes of worldwide rising expectations are advertising, movies, television, magazines, education, and travel to foreign lands. The problem is that when rising expectations are not met, rebellion occurs.

It is no longer enough that a manager master the dynamics of production and marketing. Tomorrow's executives must understand the socioeconomic environment in which their companies operate. Only then can they safely chart a future course.

Cataloging of the subjects of concern to you as a manager can be quite a job. Many of them have been presented in this book. You should have the necessary information about the following areas:

- ☐ Management: organization, planning, control, decision making, legal problems, relations with government, public relations, and foreign operations.
- ☐ Personnel: selection, training, supervision, employee health, compensation, fringe benefits, job evaluation, performance appraisal, key-personnel development, and labor relations.
- ☐ The social sciences: psychology, sociology, and economics.
- ☐ Finance: sources of capital, equity capital, profits, debt, credit.
- ☐ Physical property: land, buildings, equipment, machinery, and tools.
- ☐ Methods: office procedures, costs, general accounting, budgetary control, electronic data processing.
- ☐ Production: manufacturing processes, scheduling, quality control, procurement, industrial engineering.
- ☐ Marketing: advertising, selling, distribution, marketing research, and product innovation.

## WHAT A MANAGER SHOULD DO

What should you do to become a better manager?

*Step 1. Set specific goals.* The things you do to prepare yourself for your future depend on the things you want, your inclinations. Your wants must be fairly specific. Below is a list of possible basic wants and related specific goals.

| **Basic Wants** | **Specific Goals** |
|---|---|
| Wealth | $50,000 per year |
| Possessions | A four-bedroom house |
| Power | Election as a senator |
| Fame | A best-seller novel |
| Prestige | President of a university |
| Acceptance | Member of some select club |
| To improve society | Member of a reform movement |
| To help your community | Head of a community fund |
| Creativity (manual) | To construct a coffee table |
| Creativity (mental) | To write a research report |
| Creativity (social) | To organize a club |

Can you look at the first list, select two or three basic wants that are very strong within you, and then set your own specific goals for the basic wants which drive you? If so, you have accomplished the first step of the things you should do to raise your level of preparation in management.

*Step 2. Consciously seek abounding health and energy.* You already know most of the elements which contribute to health and energy: proper diet, exercise for your age and physical condition, adequate sleep, fresh air, sunshine, rest when tired, muscular relaxation, play. To these positive influences should be added avoidance of excesses in food, alcohol, tobacco, drugs, and negative emotions.

*Step 3. Develop your mental powers.* Enlarge your vocabulary. Learn to use "power words" in your conversation. Improve your memory. Add to your knowledge of mathematics. Read widely in many fields. Check the reasoning by which you reached conclusions.

To improve your vocabulary, buy a good dictionary. Each time you come across a new word, look it up. Write it down in a small book you carry at all times. Use that word when you can reasonably do so in your conversation.

Learn to use action verbs and word-picture nouns which will energize others to favorable response. Say "galvanize to action" instead of "move," "exhilaration" instead of "satisfaction," "pawing stallion" instead of "restless horse," "gigantic challenges" instead of "big problems." Conjure up specific images in the minds of your listeners.

Power words also include "pedestal phrases," such as "because of your experience," "a man of your standing," "I need your advice." These phrases are effective because they put the other fellow up on a pedestal.

You can improve your memory by concentrating on the things you want to remember, such as a person's name. Repeat it from time to time. Notebooks, pocket memory joggers, calendar pads, and "bring-up files" can also bolster your memory.

Mathematics has become far more important in management than it was only a few years ago. Consider what kind of mathematics is important in your present job, and what kinds will be important in jobs ahead. Study how mathematics is used in business.

By reading widely in many fields, you will not only become better informed, you will also become a better conversationalist—particularly if you learn the art of being a good listener. By keeping abreast of national and international events, you will realize the importance of your job and of management in general to the welfare of the nation and the future of the world. Such realization in itself is strong motivation for you.

Much faulty reasoning results from lack of information. What you see may have various causes, not necessarily the most obvious one. Likewise something that you see happen may have many effects, some immediate, some in the future. So when you are trying to reach an important conclusion, ask the right questions, get adequate information, and consider all possible answers, not just the one you like. Peter Drucker, the management consultant, says that his job is not to give answers, but to ask the right questions. If the right questions are asked, the answers become obvious.

*Step 4. Conserve the use of your own time.* If your time is worth $15 an hour to an employer, shouldn't it be worth that much to you? If so, then each hour you waste means that you have wasted $15. Most of us believe that we could be more successful if we only had more time. Yet the most successful people in the world have exactly the same amount of time as we do. It's not the amount of time you have, but how you use your time, that counts.

Part of your time problem is to keep others from using it up. People with time on their hands usually spend it with someone who doesn't have that time. Avoid being that someone. Figure 19 will give you an opportunity to evaluate how you spend a typical day in business. Fill it out carefully, total the figures on the bottom line, and calculate the percentages. You may be shocked.

Planning what you do each day and each week can help you conserve time. If you write out your plan, you're more likely to stick to it than if you simply think about it.

*Step 5. Develop your social contacts.* Social ability is not hereditary, nor is it some God-given gift. You can develop your social ability if you really want to. You'll need to become more extrovert in your relationships with others, learn to be persuasive in those relationships, and persist in trying to accomplish your aims with others.

When you are extrovert, you like people and you like to help them. You maintain a friendly openness toward them. You avoid grudges. You pay attention to your friends and maintain your friendships.

When trying to be persuasive, you have to listen to understand the needs of others. A good salesman sells satisfaction, not merely goods. Persuasion is partly salesmanship. Here the use of power words can be helpful. Improving your communication with others is a form of self-development.

Elbert Hubbard, a homespun philosopher of a previous generation, said it as well as anyone: "The recipe for having friends is to be one." An introvert shuts others out. But the very wall that shuts them out also shuts him in.

Psychologists have a simple formula for developing extroversion: Assume a virtue whether you have it or not, and soon it will be yours. In other words, if you would be extrovert, act as an extrovert should. By doing this consistently, you will soon become genuinely extrovert.

The desire to change must come from within you. It cannot be imposed upon you. You have to believe that it is in your self-interest to change. Maybe you will realize that you are in an environment which requires new adaptations. Certainly all signs point to the present era as being one of rapid radical change.

*Figure 19. Time analysis for managers.*

Your Name ______________________ Date ______________

Using a typical day, enter the actual number of minutes each half-hour that you spend on each activity. In the blank spaces provided, enter any other activities not already listed.

| | DESK WORK | | | | | | | | | | TALKING | | | | | | | | | MISC. | | | | |
|---|---|---|---|---|---|---|---|---|---|---|---|---|---|---|---|---|---|---|---|---|---|---|---|---|
| Make entries for each half-hour beginning: | Studying correspondence | Studying reports | Clerical work | Planning | Dictation | Preparing reports | Telephoning (business) | Telephoning (personal) | Other: | Other: | Nonbusiness | With business caller | With a superior | With an associate | Supervising employees | Listening to a suggestion | Conducting a meeting | Other: | Other: | Doing physical work | Driving a car | Lunch | Other: | |
| 7:00 | | | | | | | | | | | | | | | | | | | | | | | | |
| 7:30 | | | | | | | | | | | | | | | | | | | | | | | | |
| 8:00 | | | | | | | | | | | | | | | | | | | | | | | | |
| 8:30 | | | | | | | | | | | | | | | | | | | | | | | | |
| 9:00 | | | | | | | | | | | | | | | | | | | | | | | | |
| 9:30 | | | | | | | | | | | | | | | | | | | | | | | | |
| 10:00 | | | | | | | | | | | | | | | | | | | | | | | | |
| 10:30 | | | | | | | | | | | | | | | | | | | | | | | | |
| 11:00 | | | | | | | | | | | | | | | | | | | | | | | | |
| 11:30 | | | | | | | | | | | | | | | | | | | | | | | | |
| 12:00 | | | | | | | | | | | | | | | | | | | | | | | | |
| 12:30 | | | | | | | | | | | | | | | | | | | | | | | | |
| 1:00 | | | | | | | | | | | | | | | | | | | | | | | | |
| 1:30 | | | | | | | | | | | | | | | | | | | | | | | | |
| 2:00 | | | | | | | | | | | | | | | | | | | | | | | | |
| 2:30 | | | | | | | | | | | | | | | | | | | | | | | | |
| 3:00 | | | | | | | | | | | | | | | | | | | | | | | | |
| 3:30 | | | | | | | | | | | | | | | | | | | | | | | | |
| 4:00 | | | | | | | | | | | | | | | | | | | | | | | | |
| 4:30 | | | | | | | | | | | | | | | | | | | | | | | | |
| 5:00 | | | | | | | | | | | | | | | | | | | | | | | | |
| 5:30 | | | | | | | | | | | | | | | | | | | | | | | | |
| TOTAL | | | | | | | | | | | | | | | | | | | | | | | | |
| % | | | | | | | | | | | | | | | | | | | | | | | | 100 |

Study the bottom line to determine which activities you should stress and which you should minimize in the future.

Here is a small act you can take today to start you on your way to developing extroversion. Say "good morning" to the first person you see after leaving your home, whether you know him or not.

Persistence is required in pursuit of all your aims, not just the one of raising your level of preparation in management. You don't have to do extraordinary things in your working life. Just do ordinary things extraordinarily well. Place your bets on your industriousness, not on a belief in your genius or some lucky miracle. If you keep doing little things well, soon greater things will knock at your door, begging to be done. Doing little things well promotes persistence.

Much of your success will stem from what you do after the evening meal. How will you spend those 15-dollar hours? The daily chores of common living keep sniping at your hopes and ambitions. Persistent study, as an example, requires drive and will power. A Chinese proverb says, "Great souls have wills—feeble ones have only wishes." How many people do you know who have a wishbone where their backbone should be?

In an emergency almost any human being can produce tremendous energy. The energy has been there all the time, a potential waiting for an outlet. In emergency, it explodes; in persistence, it is released drop by drop. The energy which occasionally spurts from a disorganized mind is no match for that which streams quietly from an organized mind. You can guide and control the release of your energy. To do so, it may be necessary to sacrifice some present satisfactions for future gains. You alone can decide whether it is worth it.

Don't be afraid to try new things. The humorist says you'll never stub your toe standing still, but you'll never go places either. A mistake is evidence that you tried to do something. Someone has said that success is 10 percent inspiration and 90 percent perspiration. When called a genius, the great pianist Paderewski commented, "Perhaps I am. But before I was a genius, I was a drudge." When you are faced with opportunity you may not recognize it, for it may just look like a lot of hard work.

These are the things you might do to qualify for a higher level of management than you now have achieved. However, there is another slant to this problem: what you should do for your subordinates. You can apply the principles of what you should know, do, and be to help develop subordinates.

## What You Should Be

The things you should strive to be fall into four areas:

1. You should be interested in what you are doing. Interest provides self-motivation. It adds an emotional overtone to learning and to doing.

2. You should be forceful in pursuit of your specific aims. This means you will not lose track of those aims in the busyness of daily work. It means that when decisions have to be made, you will make them in light of how they will affect your goals.

3. You should be a good supervisor. As such you will be loyal to your own boss. You will believe that he is fair and capable, that he has many problems, that he needs your help and in turn wants to help you. You will be confident that your subordinates respect you, that they want to work, that they can be trusted, and that they are capable. You will believe that you are equal to your job, that you like the work you are doing, and that you want higher responsibility. In your relationships with subordinates you will be fair, tactful, and open-minded.

4. Finally, at all times, you will strive to be emotionally mature.

It is difficult to describe emotional maturity in a few words, because it is a collection of many positive traits.

Children, when faced with threats, dangers, decisions, frustrations or when possessed by negative emotions, may exhibit immature reactions—flight, rage, attack, lies, or withdrawal. Immature adults may follow much the same patterns, sometimes disguised as boasting, putting on a tough front, timidity, jealousy, sarcasm, apple-polishing, bigotry, sabotage, alcoholism, alibis, and feelings of persecution and guilt.

You have long heard about the Holy Trinity—but there is an *unholy* trinity: hate, fear, and guilt. Hate shows itself in many forms: sarcasm, ridicule, envy, jealousy, revenge, gossip, innuendo, intolerance, cruelty. Fear masquerades as aggression, insecurity, timidity, flight, indecisiveness, superstitions, phobias, anxiety, sycophancy, inferiority, and overassertiveness. Guilt may manifest itself as vain regrets, depression, martyrdom, secretiveness, and oversensitivity.

Medical experts tell us that when any of these negative emotions possess us, harm results to the body and peace of mind is impossible.

For the duration of the emotion we are emotionally immature.

The person who is emotionally mature bases his conclusions on facts, not hunches. He faces problems and dangers with courage, meets his responsibilities, makes his own decisions. He is patient, persistent, tactful, tolerant, forgiving, and willing to compromise. He plans his activities and pursues them vigorously. Physically relaxed, he enjoys peace of mind most of the time. His opponents find it difficult to withstand a man who has already conquered himself.

Many strong leaders have been emotionally immature—usually showing signs of paranoia. They have ridden rough-shod over their fellows. Many have torn themselves apart with negative emotions. Their breed is disappearing in industrial leadership.

You live according to your needs, your standards, your beliefs. To raise them to higher levels, you require (1) dissatisfaction with your present condition, (2) specific short- and long-range goals, and (3) the mental and physical drive to change your living habits.

Leaders of the future will be men of vision. They will believe that the present is but prologue to a greater future. They will want to be a contributing part of that future.

Thomas Jefferson once wrote, "I like the dreams of the future better than the history of the past." Leaders of the future will subscribe to the philosopher who said, "Dream no little dreams; they have no power to stir the imaginations of men." Wasn't it Robert Kennedy who said, "Some people see things as they are and ask, 'Why?' I dream of things that have never been and ask, 'Why not?' "

## The Four Factors of Success

Some years ago a large company engaged the author's consulting firm to find out why so many of its middle managers were failing. The study stretched over many months. Scores of individuals were interviewed or observed in action. Their backgrounds were studied. Some reasons for failing were company deficiencies, but most causes were defects in the individuals themselves. When finally we classified our findings, we called our report *The Four Factors of Success.* Serious violations of some of these factors contributed to failure. Here are the four factors, with important subdivisions:

1. *Character:* intellectual honesty, perseverance, loyalty, faith, integrity, acceptance of responsibility.

2. *Temperament:* equanimity, emotional maturity, adaptability, poise, patience, mental peace.

3. *Ability:* physical, intellectual, vocational, social. Each of these areas in turn has many subdivisions:

a. physical—health, energy, diet, weight, exercise, sleep.
b. intellectual—memory, mathematics, vocabulary, space perception, reasoning.
c. vocational—technical knowledge, skills, experience.
d. social—extroversion, dominance, tact, listening, communication.

4. *Interest:* emotional satisfaction from working with people, or ideas, or mathematics, or physical objects. For example, if a mechanical genius had to sell, or to supervise employees, he would be working in an area from which he derived no interest and chances are he would become a failure.

Many successful executives lack some of these traits but compensate with an abundance of other positive attributes. Nevertheless, even successful managers can benefit from a study of the above factors of success.

This book has endeavored to bring out the principal viewpoints and techniques of modern management, to forecast its near-term future, and to suggest how you can become part of that future. What you do with these ideas now rests in your hand.

## REVIEW

What new things should a future manager study?

Name some actions which a manager should take now to prepare for managing in the near future.

What are the three areas of the "unholy trinity"?

What are the four major factors of success?

In what way, if any, has this book altered the outlook for your future?

# INDEX

employee relations, 98–112